The Unexpected Kitchen

ITALIAN CUISINE
& OTHER DELICIOUS RECIPES

A Recipe Collection
by **Sara Ciliberto**

Copyright © 2023
Concetta "Sara" Ciliberto
& The Unexpected Kitchen, LLC
All rights reserved.
ISBN: 979-8-9893789-3-7

The Unexpected Kitchen

ITALIAN CUISINE
& OTHER DELICIOUS RECIPES

SARA CILIBERTO

table of contents

an introduction to Sara & The Unexpected Kitchen

notes before cooking, Sara's Way

antipasto :: appetizers, 1

primo :: first course, 15

secondo :: second course, 63

sugo :: sauce, 79

contorno :: side dishes, 89

pane :: bread, 105

insalata :: salads, 115

dolce :: dessert, 129

cin cin!

an introduction to Sara

"Make sure you comb your little sister's hair,
wash her face, & put her dress on,
okay Sara?"

Those were the last words I heard from my Mother's voice, before she got on that train, on November 17, 1951. It has been 72 years since her death & I still feel it like it was yesterday.

I have an older sister, Melina, who is nine years older than me. At the time, she was 18 years old & had just become a teacher. The state hired her one town over from where we lived & would commute by train. And because she was only 18, my mom took the train with her on this day.

"A mother & daughter go out of town..." read the headlines, after the *Ciliberto Bridge* collapsed in Italia, killing several on the train that drove over it that day, which included my Mother.

At home, my little sister's dress laid out on the bed, just how my Mom left it.

It was still war time in Italia so my Papa was in Argentina. And now, Melina, one of the few survivors of the accident, would spend the next year in the hospital. At the age of nine years old, I was left to care for my older brother, Rocco, & little sister, Paola.

My Zia Antonietta was our only relative that lived close by. But she would cook for my sister, Melina, & walk four miles to the hospital to see her, almost everyday. I thank her for looking after us & for taking care of Melina during that time.

But otherwise, the three of us were alone. Right away, I had to start figuring out meals for my brother and sister. And we did not have too much. It was war time, think about it. We only had what the American airplanes used to throw down to us. And then we'd go out and into the mountains to see what we could find to take home.

My Mom always said to us, "don't take nothing from anyone, we are not poor." We *were* poor. And people knew that my Mom was a very proud woman. So after the accident, all the neighbors would come and leave food at the steps of our house. They left us chestnuts, pears, broccoli, and potatoes. Anything they brought from the fields, they used to leave some for me.

After they'd leave, I'd run down there & pick up the food. And then, I'd start cooking. That's how it all came about.

But even so, I thought, how am I going to cook? I never saw my Mom even cook! After she died, I remembered the potatoes. They were always there in a basket. And onions. And we always had oil, too. I don't know where it came from, but there was always oil in a jar.

We used to have a fire 'stove,' which consisted of an iron tripod over a fire. And then, we put the frying pan on top.

So, the first time I remember, in those first few days, I cut up the potato in circles & then the onion, put a little oil in the pan, & it cooked.

And it was delicious.

The next day, I said to myself, now what am I going to do with this potato? This time, I chopped it & made little tiny squares.

After that, I cooked those potatoes and onions in so many different ways.

That's when, I think, the 'creativity' came about. Today, even, my potatoes, I cook them in so many different ways & shapes & each time, they become a different, beautiful plate!

In the end, my creativity came from the need to prepare food. The need to prepare food for me, my brother, and sister. We didn't have any other way. Whether or not I knew how, at the age of nine years old, I needed to cook for them. And that's the beauty of it. That's why I'm so passionate about food and sometimes why I can quickly become so emotional about it, too.

Photo Credit: Mario Elias Muñoz Valencia, *Mestock*, Spain, September 2022

Once Paola & Rocco went off to their schools, I went to stay with my Zia Isabella, who lived a lot further away, but only for a few months. I thank her, too, for taking care of me.

When Melina got out of the hospital after the train accident & went back to teaching, she became a third grade teacher in one of the nearby towns. I was about ten, going on eleven, when that winter, she got so sick. She had a fever, about 40C or 104F. So she says to me, "I'm really sick, Sara. You need to go talk to the landlords and see if they can give us a chicken so you can make soup. Otherwise, I'm not going to make it."

So, I went out to find the landlords, but couldn't find them. Now, the chickens were walkin' around, but not a soul was out that day. I went back home, "Melina, they're not there." She said, "Okay, did you see any chickens?" I said, yeah. "Okay, you need to go and grab a chicken. You need to make soup for me!" I went out again & tried chasing after the chickens but they kept running away from me! I went back to my sister again. "Okay. I know you cannot grab the chicken because they run away...just hit it with something! With a stone...anything!" Again, I went out.

I saw one little stool, where one of our landlords used to sit and roll her silk. I used to help her sometimes. I grabbed that little stool and I threw it at the chicken, and looked the other way. When I looked back, the chicken did not move. So, I picked it up and took it back home.

There are angels all around us. And I do believe in them. But that poor baby...life made me do it! And I was sick to my stomach about it.

When I got back, I said to Melina, "Now, what do I do with this?" With a fever, she directed me with what to do next, step by step. Pull this and pull that, she said. I don't even need to close my eyes as I tell you this, I can feel myself pulling out every one of those feathers still today!

I made the soup, her fever came down, & she was better the next day.

Melina, Me, My Mom, Paola, & Rocco

After the fifth grade in Italia, we went to Argentina to be with my Dad. Melina stayed in Italia to work. Fifth grade would be the end of my education. But, living in Italia & then Argentina, I now speak Italian & Spanish!

Monday through Saturday, my brother, Rocco, would go to work & my little sister went to school. I stayed home and cooked. Papa used to give me money, I would do the shopping, figure out how much we could spend, & then I did the cooking. I was like the lady of the house!

Sundays, we all had the day 'off.'

Sundays were for my Dad to cook. He was passionate about cooking. I remember on those Sundays, we would get up & go to church. When we'd come back, he'd turn on some opera music, & start making his sauce. If we tried to help, he would tell us, "No no, rest!" On Sundays, all Dad wanted was for us to just relax. The end result? All of us as a family, enjoying 'My Father's Sunday Sauce.'

Paola, my Papa, Rocco, Me

When I was about 15 years old, I needed a job! The town where my Papa lived didn't have any jobs for me. But there were jobs in the town where Zia Antonietta moved to. So I moved in with her, my uncle, & my four cousins...and Paola & Rocco came with me!

My Zia Antonietta now had to cook for 10 people, twice a day, every single day. She would go to the mercado at the end of the day to take home the damaged produce, like bruised tomatoes.

Meanwhile, on my way home from work, I would pass by the mercado, seeing all the fresh flowers. I'd take home one or two & give them to Zia Antonietta who was working so hard to feed us all. Buying those flowers gave me happiness. It's what kept me alive, I think.

"I know they look beautiful, but we cannot eat flowers," she would say to me when I'd get home, putting my flower into a little vase next to the plates. Meaning, stop spending the money on flowers...we need to eat! She'd ask me to try whatever she was making, "what do you think, Sara?" About the flavors & what she was cooking. To watch another woman cook and to have another woman to look up to, like Melina, my Zia Antonietta also became like another Mother to me.

I was still in Argentina when I was about to turn 21. I had promised Melina back in Italia, that when I became 21, I would go visit. So leading up to my birthday, I made sure to make enough money to pay for my trip. By then, I had become a dress designer & was working three jobs.

Three days before I had planned to leave for my trip, we were having dinner. I had an envelope leaning up against my drinking glass. Inside the envelope held my round-trip ticket to Italia. We were eating when finally one of my cousins asked me to pass down the envelope to see what was in it. "This is a joke, right...?" they said, "how did you...?!"

Because without asking for money, without getting any help from anyone, I paid for my ticket myself. Three days later, I left Argentina.

Three days before I left Italia to come back to Argentina, I met John Ciliberto. In those three days, he told me he had fallen in love with me & wanted to marry me! I said, "No! My family is in Argentina, I have to go back!"

Let's just say he never gave up. We got married less than four months later.

John would end up giving me his last name, Ciliberto, the same as the name of the bridge where my Mom died. How do you explain *that!*

Since the very beginning, my house has always been open for friends & family. Through the years with John, sometimes our friends would call us & say, *guys, let's go out for dinner, there's a new restaurant that just opened up.* I used to say, *why go there?...come here!*

I still have a friend from when John & I lived in Long Grove, Illinois. He was one of our neighbors & now, one of my viewers. Every now and then, he sends me a little note, "Sara, I look at your food, & I feel like you're still here. But then I look at your old house & there's no smell coming out, because you're not here."

After my husband died, my son said to me, *Mom, you have to take care of yourself. You did everything for him! You have to learn how to be happy the way you are.*

When John was alive, I guess you could say I had a purpose. We'd get up every morning & he used to say to me while we were drinking our coffee, "Okay, Sara, what are we eating tonight?" I'd say, "John, I'll let you know at five o'clock, okay?" I'm not thinking about dinner in the morning! First, we have to do breakfast and then we do lunch. And up until dinner, I had my job, because I was a designer with three stores. So I told him, "after I close up the stores, I'll let you know. Just don't worry, John. You're gonna eat!"

That was everyday, for 55 years, with John. Not just one day and not just every month. Every. Day.

And for me, having that 'never get tired of cooking' feeling was because of the delicious appetite he had for Italian Cuisine. His friends used to say to him, 'when you marry Sara, you win the lotto,' because I always fed him well & he used to smile because of it. If I did not have a man that appreciated food and had the palette for what I cooked for him...I don't think any woman would cook! By asking me every morning, over our morning coffee, *what are you making for dinner, Sara?*, he gave me the energy to cook. So, I would suggest, to any man reading this book; if you like when your wife cooks, be enthusiastic about it! I appreciated it. So go into that kitchen every once in a while and say, 'mmmm, it smells so good in here!' You will make your wife feel so good that she'll get up tomorrow morning and think, 'hmm, I wonder what I can make for this man today?'

For 55 years, that was my reason to get up in the morning.

so, I'd like to dedicate this book...

To life.

To my Mother that I did not know,
other than the smell of her home baked bread coming out of the oven.
I can still smell it today.

To my older sister, Melina,
who, to me, was the perfect picture of a sister.
Beautiful & intelligent, but also who became my Mother for a short time.

To my little sister, Paola,
who, today, is still a better cook than me.

To my Father, my Papa,
& his sauce on Sundays.

To my brother, Rocco,
who always appreciated the aroma coming into my house
& the taste of my food.

To my husband, John,
who lived everyday just so he could sit down
and eat that meal I cooked for him.

To my friends,
who walk into my house and appreciate, no matter what I make.
It could be a disaster & they still eat it.

To life.

To the men of my life.
My husband,
Giovani Battista Ciliberto II,
my son,
Giovan Battista Ciliberto III,
my grandson,
John Dominico,
my brother,
Rocco.
& my cousin,
Rocco.

To my special friend, Dan, who with his desire & palette for good food, gave me the strength to start cooking again after my Johnny died.

And to my dear friends, Rebecca, Jill, Caroline, & Maura, for leading me back to life again.

"But I don't feel like going," I said, when my friend Rebecca came to pick me up one night. "Get ready, I'm not leaving until you come with me," she said.

That night, I met Jill, to whom, a little while later, I said, "I'm so bored...doing dresses is not enough stimulation, I need to cook. Come over for dinner...and bring your friends!"

After I lost Johnny, I lost that purpose in the morning. No one to cook for. No one to ask me, what are you making for dinner tonight, Sara?

I needed people in my house. And I wanted to cook.

One night, with about 6 or 7 women at my house, my friend Maura said, "let's go live!" So we went live on Facebook that night while I cooked for everyone.

'Sara Cooking With Friends' became 'The Unexpected Kitchen,' and we started our live cooking show in June 2018. Shortly after, I opened my home to private cooking classes.

Since then, happiness has been brought back into my home & I've become alive again. My friends, my family, my viewers, they all give me so much. It's because of them, that when I wake up in the morning now, I get to ask myself, what am I going to make this week?

Thank you all, my friends,
for all that you did to help me out of the most difficult time of my life.

And to my family.

Thank you, thank you.

& lastly, to my home country of Italia

The most important town in my life is Vena Superiore,
the little town where I was born.

Vibo Valentia,
where my sister, Melina, still lives today.

Curinga,
where my father was born and where my Zia Isabella used to live,
where she took care of me for that little while.

Jacurso,
the town where my husband, John, was born.
Where I learned how to make homemade salami, prosciutto, capocollo,
& where I learned how to make zeppole for the first time.

Tropea & Capo Vaticano,
where John & I used to visit every year for 55 years.
We used to go up the mountains & pick the green peas, fava beans, & fresh wild strawberries. We'd get the chestnuts, the almonds, figs, every kind of fig you could imagine from all the fig trees. Every 3-4 days, we'd go from the mountains down to Capo Vaticano, the beach! My husband loved the mountains but I loved the beach. But by going back and forth, we got to try so many different foods. The mountain food was more rustic where the food at the beach was just fresh, fresh everything,
just how I like it!

an introduction to The Unexpected Kitchen

Today, you go to the store & you buy the little basil on the shelf, right? A few little leaves in this little tiny package. And it costs you $3 to $5. Then, the next day when you need it, it's already spoiled & you have to throw it away! So many years ago, I decided to dry my own spices. My husband, John, always tended to the garden that we cultivated together so I already had the fresh herbs. Now, I was drying my own spices. After that, came my organically infused olive oil.

Everyone that came to my house, they loved my food! A lot of the time, I was using my infused olive oil & dried spices. They'd say how much they loved it so I'd give them a little jar of it to take home. Day by day, everyone said my food tasted so different. So, not too long ago, I decided to package it up & sell it.

Unexpectedly.

I never had the idea to sell my infused olive oil or dried spices, until one particular person came over for dinner. He was a doctor, local to where I live now. We had appetizers & he brought over a few delicious cheeses & divine wine. At the end of the night, he said, *Sara, I love that olive oil that you use to serve the bruschetta & I love your dipping oil. Before I go home, make sure you tell me the brand because I'd like to give it to all my friends for Christmas.*

At the end of the night, I went to my pantry & gave him one of my bottles, which at the time, didn't have anything on the front of them. "Take this one," I said. "No, no, I don't want yours, I just want the brand name of the one you buy." He proceeded to tell me how he was a connoisseur of olive oil, buying all the best olive oils from around the world, like Spain, Turkey, Greece, & even Italia.

Meanwhile, my heart is pumping out of my chest! Nervously, I took the bottle to him & said, "Here. No brand. You can't buy this anywhere."
"Well…you *must* bring this to the market then," he said.

And me, in my head, I told myself he was right. I *gotta* do it.

He put me in touch with someone to formally establish once and for all, The Unexpected Kitchen. I saw him maybe once or twice after that & never saw him again.

And so, The Unexpected Kitchen was born.

That's such a hard name, Sara, no one is going to remember it! Those are some of the things people said when I chose the name, The Unexpected Kitchen. So I say to them, I'm not doing this to be an easy name. The Unexpected Kitchen came about because that's who I am. Unexpected Sara! In the spur of the moment, if it's six o'clock & ten people call me & ask if they can stop by? Well, sure! But now, what am I going to feed them? And that's when I open my fridge and whatever I have, I prepare. And what I create? Always unexpected.

All the way from that little tripod stove over the fire & my potatoes & onions, The Unexpected Kitchen has brought me nothing but positives. I couldn't find anything negative if I tried. In fact, it actually brought me more of what I always had, a live representation of my transition from youth to becoming a mature woman to then becoming a married woman & a business woman. Now, I'm in my eighties, still being creative, & still creating the unexpected, with oils and spices that I've been using all my life.

But, the greatest achievement of all would be this. If I could convince you to use *fresh*. Fresh oil & fresh spices. If I could convince you not only of how delicious your food could taste, but how beautiful your food will look & how good you might feel!

As of the making of this book, I am 81 years old. I take one teaspoon of my organic, first-pressed infused olive oil every morning before my coffee. I take no medication & my blood pressure is great. I move about & never sit too long. Because here's one thing, you cannot just sit and pretend that you're going to get up. Go move your body. And your brain. Because when you move your body, you move your brain, and you keep thinking so you keep creating!

So, my friends, I hope that by using the best oils & the best spices & fresh fruits & colorful veggies, that we all get to live long, healthy, happy lives together, okay? Alla salute!

To all my friends who give me such great testimonials,
thank you for watching me from around the world.
You all make me smile.

Sara's Way
notes before cooking

People often come to my cooking classes & say, *it tastes so good, Sara, can I have the recipe?* So I give them the recipe. Then, they go home with the recipe, the same way we did it during the class. But then they say, *mine doesn't taste the same.* So I say, *well, did you use the good olive oil that I gave you? The good salt? The spices that I gave you in the little baggy?*

My friends, you need to put the flavors in when you cook. You can use whatever veggies you want & you can chop them in any shape that you like. But, the flavors, the herbs, the spices, & the oils, that's how you make a different dish.

Now, when you are in the kitchen, like I tell all my viewers, be your own queen! Do whatever you want! You are the queen & nobody can take that away from you. And if they don't want to be there, kick 'em out. Tell 'em to come back when the food is ready.

There is no school to tell you how to chop this or that or even how much. To me, that's what I love most about what I do. I cook with my eyes. I pick up a zucchini or a potato & do whatever comes from my brain or what mood I'm in. It doesn't matter. The thing that matters is the act of putting it together, putting the flavors in, putting in lots and lots of love, and feeding your friends & family!

Remember, food tastes good when you put good quality into it. For me, when I feed my guests in my house, I want them to have the best & I want them to feel their best. Use the very best quality that you can, when you can. But at the very least, use the best olive oil & the freshest herbs & spices!

So, my friends, I introduce to you, "Sara's Way!" If you want to pack the flavor the way that I do, here are a few things to expect while you're working through my recipes. But remember, this is just how I do it in my kitchen. I am the queen of my kitchen. Be the queen of yours! Be spontaneous. Add your own swing however you want, whenever you want!

Salt & Pepper
First & foremost, I always cook with pink himalayan sea salt. When I don't have any, I use white sea salt. Also, I like to have a jar of pink salt combined with black pepper so that it's one less step in the kitchen when I'm cooking with both.

Oven & Stove Temperatures
When you are cooking my recipes or even any others, make sure you consider that the strength of my oven or stove could be very different than the strength of yours. Please adjust accordingly.

Italian Parsley
When I use parsley, I only use 'Italian flat leaf parsley.' That's my preference. When mentioned in my recipes, know that it's Italian parsley.

Tomatoes
When using tomatoes, I always remove all the seeds & all the juices. The only exception is cherry tomatoes, I keep them as they are. So, if you're making one of my recipes that call for plum or large tomatoes, I would advise you to do the same. It really does make a big difference. When I make my marinara sauce, people say to me, "Sara, is your sauce naturally sweet or do you use sugar?" No sugar in Sara's marinara sauce. Don't put the acid in from the tomatoes & you won't have to put sugar in it to sweeten it. That's my way of doing it. When tomatoes are mentioned in my recipes, with the exception of cherry tomatoes, this is the protocol to follow.

Rinsing Fruits & Vegetables
Before using, I always soak my fruits & vegetables in a bath of baking soda & water. If I have the time, for at least thirty minutes. But always at least a quick rinse with the baking soda & dried completely with a towel. Do this for all recipes in this book!

Rinsing Meats
I know I'm going to make a lot of people mad with this one, especially the professional chefs, but this is Sara's Way! When I cook chicken, turkey, liver, or sausage with casing, I always soak in white vinegar & water for at least 10-20 minutes & pat dry. When I do this, I feel like I'm cleansing my meat of any impurities & before even cooking them, I've already given them some good, clean flavor. Just try it, okay?

TUK Olive Oil *(Olive Oil from The Unexpected Kitchen)*
If I am using olive oil, I am always, 100% of the time, using the olive oil that I infuse myself & sell at *The Unexpected Kitchen.* I infuse organic, first-pressed olive oil with fresh herbs & spices. You can purchase my olive oil at my website anytime. But if you choose to use something different, use the very best olive oil, extra extra virgin if you can!

TUK Dried Spices *(Dried Spices from The Unexpected Kitchen)*
Use the fresh spices, my friends. Fresh thyme, oregano, fennel, rosemary, parsley, cilantro, mint, sage, all of them. What these spices can do for you. Spices give us life! At *The Unexpected Kitchen,* I also dry & sell my own spices. If you use them, you only need a sprinkle of them because they are very strong & packed with flavor. Unless you are coating with my dried spices, then absolutely, you can use generously.

Pasta
I buy Italian pasta whenever I can. No enriched or bleached flour & always pale in color. I also prefer to use durum wheat semolina pasta whenever possible. If you use the good pasta, not only will you be feeding yourself, your friends, & family with the best, but you shouldn't have to rinse it! Also, get yourself a pasta straining spoon. That way, you can keep the pasta water right there on the stove to use until you're done cooking. So much easier & quicker. Lastly, when making homemade pasta, and for the recipes in this book, a general rule of thumb is to use 1 egg for each person. If you're cooking for four, use four eggs. And the flour? Use as much as it takes. And remember, al dente, always!

The Eye Emphasizes the Taste
People eat with their eyes, it's true! Food needs to look attractive. That's what I'm here to emphasize. Say you've made something so simple, like hamburgers, but you want to eat from paper plates. That's fine! But first, put your burgers on a nice big plate. For me, I think a great big white oval platter makes food look so much better! Try it for yourself. Lay out the browned hamburger buns with slices of tomato, white & purple onion, & some leafy green romaine lettuce. Then, check your fridge & see what produce you have leftover. Lay a few stalks of green onion along the platter and sprinkle some black, kalamata olives around the edges. It's going to look so nice & your guests will say, "Mmmm, I want to take a bite out of that! It looks like a million dollars!" Because it looks attractive. And then, fine, you can serve your burgers on your paper plates after that.

Make It Your Own
When you cook, no matter whose recipe you follow, try to make it your own. I may feel like using a teaspoon of salt but maybe you feel like using just a pinch. Close your eyes and go with your feelings. Your body will take you where you need to go. Make it your own & substitute. If you don't have fresh basil, use parsley. Use my idea, sure, but create it or plate it in your own way.

Fresh, Fresh, Fresh
To all my friends, decorate your kitchens with fresh, colorful, vibrant fruits, vegetables, & herbs. If you buy it & keep it in front of you, you'll use it! Try different things to keep your produce from going to waste. Roast your peppers when they start to soften. Grill the zucchini or asparagus instead of throwing them away. Make an apple tart when your apples start to wilt. Garnish your lunch or dinner with the last of your fresh basil. Fresh, fresh, fresh! Not only will you & your food be beautiful, but you will feel so good, too.

Cin Cin, my friends!
And welcome to *The Unexpected Kitchen.*
Whatever we're cooking, we're cooking it together!

*but first,
a walk through sara's garden...*

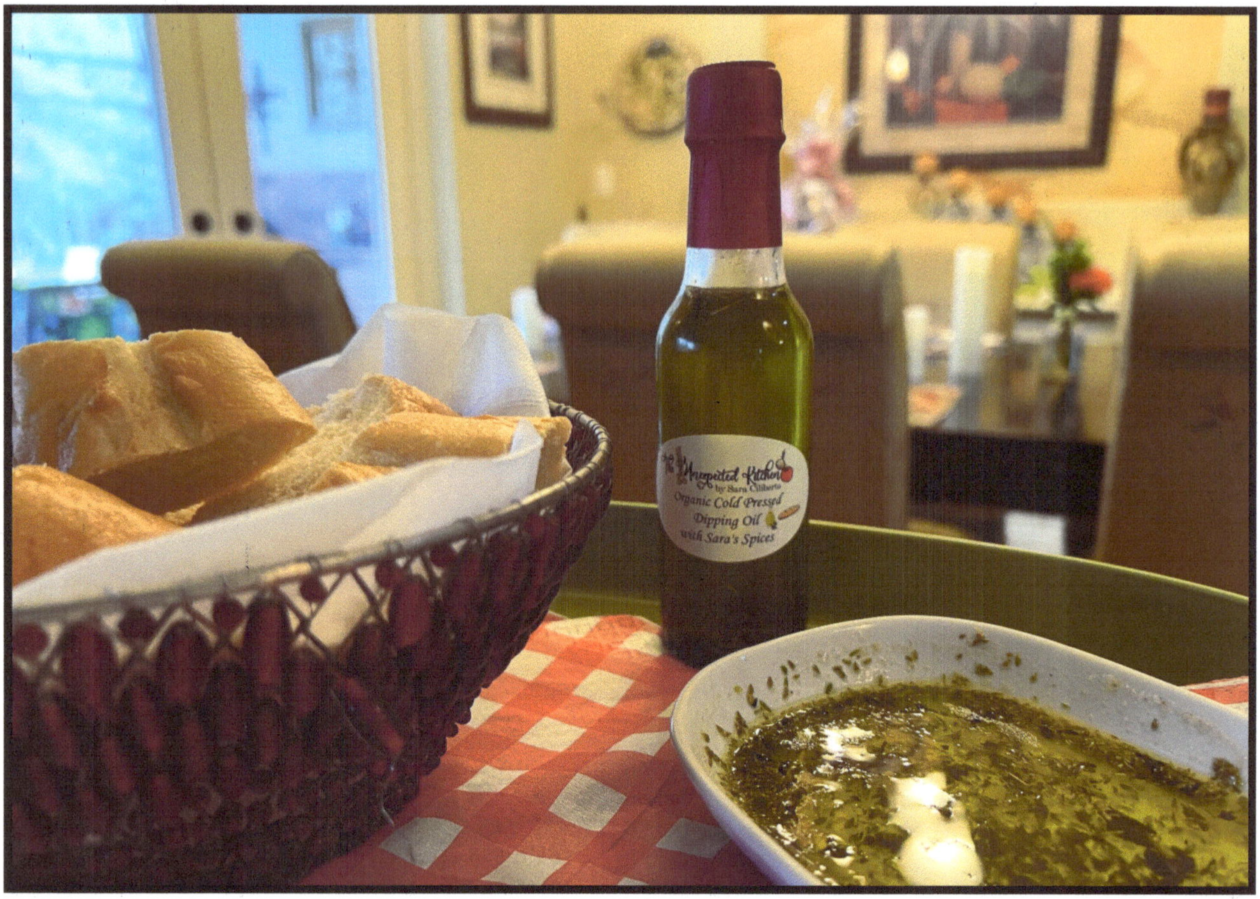
Unexpected Kitchen
Organic Cold Pressed
Dipping Oil
with Sara's Spices

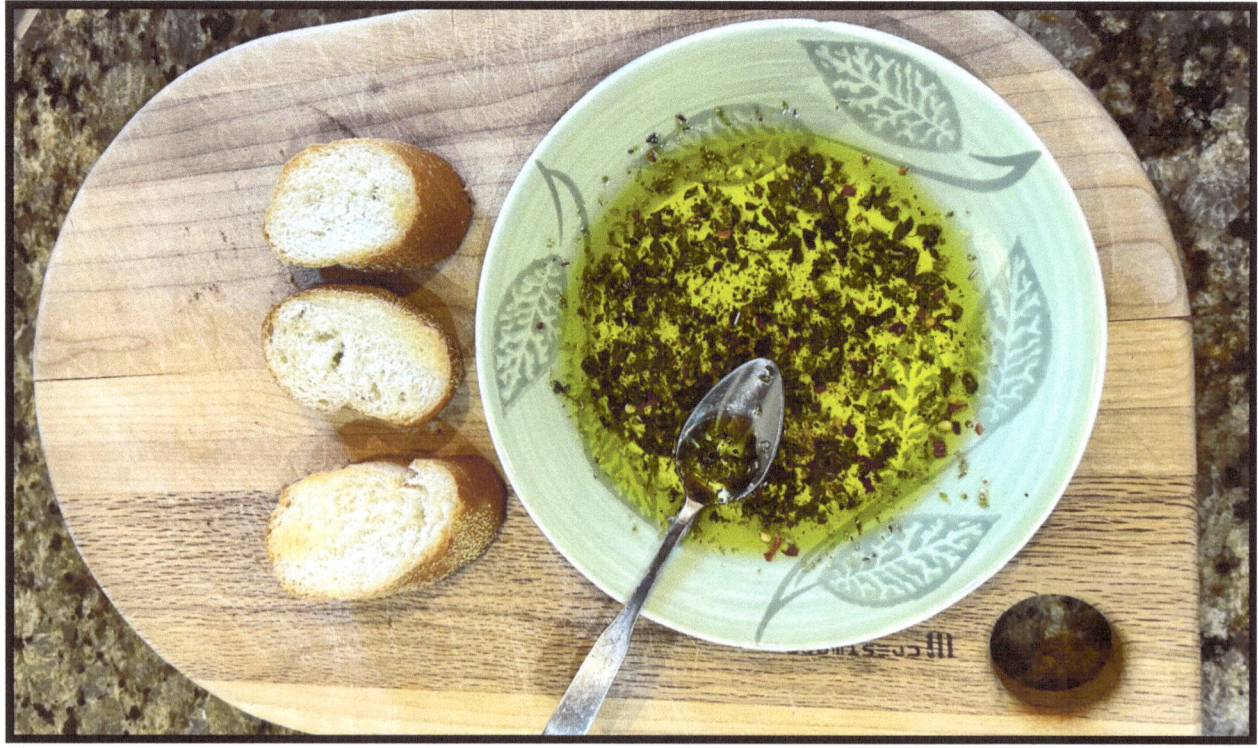

BREAD & OIL

The Unexpected Kitchen way!

INGREDIENTS

Italian Bread
Optional:
1 clove fresh garlic

TUK Dipping Oil
TUK Dried Spices
Pink salt & black pepper

DIRECTIONS

Yes, bread & oil, so simple, yet classic. And here is 'Sara's Way.'

Slice your Italian bread into ½ inch thick pieces & toast.
It is only optional that you peel a clove of fresh garlic & rub the top of your toast with the garlic.

Take a small plate & pour about 1 tbsp of TUK Dried Spices. Then, pour 2-4 tbsp of TUK Dipping Oil on top. Now, pour a little pink salt into your hand. Find the really big, beautiful grains of pink salt & add them to your dish. Finish it off with a dash of freshly ground or cracked black pepper.

That's how I do 'bread & oil.' Give it a try, my friends, & see how you like it!

BELGIUM ENDIVES

INGREDIENTS

6-9 boston endive
¼ cup pine nuts
1 cup mayonnaise
1 cup bleu cheese crumbles

DIRECTIONS

Separate your endives & wash.
Arrange & prepare your endives to be filled.

In a bowl, mix together your mayonnaise, pine nuts, & bleu cheese.
Use a spoon to fill each of your endives delicately with the mixture.
Once all are filled, arrange beautifully on a large platter.

BRACIOLE DI PATATE
potato croquettes
A traditional Calabrese dish for Sundays with family & friends.

INGREDIENTS

5-6 pounds white potatoes	3 whole eggs
1 cup all-purpose flour	1 cup fresh mozzarella
1 cup breadcrumbs	1 cup pecorino romano
½ cup canola oil	1 cup parmigiano reggiano
½ cup TUK Olive Oil	Pink salt & black pepper
4 cloves fresh garlic	*Fresh herbs:*
	Italian parsley

DIRECTIONS

If using fresh potatoes, boil, peel, mash, & place into a large mixing bowl. Finely chop all garlic & parsley. Slice your mozzarella. Then, prepare a deep frying pan over medium heat.

Mix eggs into your potatoes. Add garlic, parsley, pecorino romano, & ½ of your flour. Mix all together. Add a little breadcrumbs if too mushy.

Have two plates ready, one with ½ cup flour, & the other with 1 cup breadcrumbs & 1 cup parmigiano reggiano mixed together. *For even more flavor, sprinkle your flour with a little parmigiano reggiano, pink salt, & black pepper.*

Then, using your hands & a spoon, take a spoonful of mixture & mold with your hands into a ladyfinger shape. Press one slice of mozzarella into the center & close it back up. Roll onto flour, then breadcrumbs mixed with parmigiano reggiano, reinforce the shape, & set aside to rest. Do this with all of your mixture. Keep in fridge for at least ½ hour before frying. It will hold much better.

When you are ready to fry, add ½ cup canola & ½ cup olive oil to your hot frying pan. With this next step, be sure not to burn your oil…or your croquettes! Cook them all very slow on a gentle medium heat until thoroughly golden & crispy on the outside. Place all fried croquettes on a paper towel to absorb excess oil. Then, put on a plate & garnish with something beautiful – create your way!

BRUSCHETTA

INGREDIENTS

¼ red onion
¼ yellow bell pepper
A few cherry tomatoes
¼ cup kalamata olives
A handful of capers
A few fresh pearls of mozzarella, small

Pink salt & black pepper
TUK Dried Spices
TUK Olive Oil
Italian baguette or loaf
Fresh herbs:
Basil

DIRECTIONS

Prepare a pan over medium-high heat while you chop your red onion & yellow pepper. Cut each of the cherry tomatoes in half. Combine all in a bowl. Slice your Italian bread, about 1/2 inch thick per piece.

Add a few tablespoons of olive oil to your hot pan. Add in your veggies for a few moments, moving them around with a spatula. After a few minutes, add your kalamata olives, capers, pink salt, black pepper, & a dash of dried spices. Cook for another few minutes & then add your fresh leaves of basil & a handful of mozzarella pearls. Let cook for a moment but do not overcook!

When hot bruschetta mixture is ready, remove from pan & set aside. Then, while the pan is still hot, add your Italian bread to toast. Flip when toasted. You want it nice & crispy. Once crispy on both sides, use a spoon to cover your toasted Italian bread with the hot bruschetta mixture.

Beautify your plate with some fresh basil and please enjoy.

A classic! Plum tomatoes, feta cheese, beautiful Kalamata olives, & fresh basil, wilting away from delicious TUK Olive Oil. Finish with a dash of TUK Dried Spices & wow!

You can do so many things with these colorful bell peppers. Pickle, roast, or grill them. But don't waste! Drizzle with TUK Hot Olive Oil for a kick, & don't forget the fresh basil.

Fresh figs from my fig tree with slices of prosciutto. A delicious snack or appetizer. Don't forget to add a drizzle of raw honey on top when plated.

Perfect for summer! Slices of sweet cantaloupe wrapped in savory thin prosciutto, served on a large, white oval platter, my favorite! Decorate your plate with fresh Italian parsley.

SARA'S SPINACH DIP

INGREDIENTS

2 cups frozen spinach
3 green onions
2 cups mayonnaise
A few hearts of celery, with leaves

Celery salt
½ cup pecorino romano
1 loaf sweet Hawaiian bread

DIRECTIONS

Very finely chop the green onion, separating the whites from the greens. In a small mixing bowl, combine your whites with the mayonnaise.

Defrost your frozen spinach & squeeze out all of the excess water.

Prepare a pan over medium heat.

Take your sweet Hawaiian loaf & cut the top off. Shred the top into pieces. Remove the insides of the loaf & shred. Place all sweet Hawaiian shreds around the loaf for dipping.

To a hot pan, add ¼ cup of olive oil. When ready, sauté greens only of your green onions. Once sautéed, add spinach until fully cooked together.

When done, fully drain all oil & juice from the sautéed mixture. Then, add to the mayonnaise. Add pecorino romano & a dash of celery salt and mix together completely. Add this mixture into the Hawaiian loaf for serving.

Garnish your spinach dip with celery leaves to make it beautiful. Delicious!

PRIMO

I've been making this soup since I was 10 years old. This soup means a lot to me because it makes people feel better! When I chop all the veggies & I sauté them & cook them, & with all the feeling I put into it, I always feel like the people who eat it are going to be cured!

Now, of course, after 70 years, I have changed the recipe. After that incident with that chicken, let's just say Sara's 'Medicinal' Soup is only fresh veggies & herbs now. And of course, olive oil!

I'd like to dedicate this soup to my family & all my special friends.

I made this soup for my husband, my brother, & my son whenever they were sick.

I made this soup for my friend, Jill, when she was very ill, & my friend Bethany, too. And for my friends, Caroline & Sam, during COVID-19, who gave this soup its name.

And now, today, my son makes this soup for his kids, my two beautiful grandchildren.

SARA'S 'MEDICINAL' SOUP

INGREDIENTS

½ cup uncooked orzo
2 gold medium potatoes
1 large zucchini
1 large yellow squash
2 large carrots
3 celery stalks
¼ white cabbage
¼ green cabbage
2 cups dandelion
1 white onion
2 small plum tomatoes

Optional:
1 cup green swiss chard
Pink salt & black pepper
TUK Olive Oil
Fresh herbs:
Basil
Fennel
Italian parsley
Mint
Oregano
Rosemary

DIRECTIONS

For just the orzo, bring a small pot of salted water to a boil. In the meantime, chop all of your veggies. Peel your potatoes & chop. And last, chop all of your herbs -- except your rosemary, leave whole.

Prepare a 6-8qt pot over medium heat. Once hot, coat the bottom with olive oil.
Add cabbage, potatoes, celery, onion, carrot, tomatoes, & all herbs including full rosemary. Cook for 2-3 minutes. Add pink salt, black pepper, & fennel. Cook for another few minutes. Add zucchini, squash, dandelion, & optional swiss chard.

Sauté & move around gently. Do not destroy the natural shape of any of your ingredients.
Then, cover all ingredients with water. Let cook for about 15 minutes on low to medium heat, covered.

When ready to serve, finish with pink salt & black pepper to taste.

Drain your orzo fully. I prefer to let mine dry completely & serve separately from my soup but you can add into your soup if you'd like.

CAVATELLI

Using only two ingredients!

INGREDIENTS

2 cups all-purpose flour   1 cup warm water

DIRECTIONS

Sift all your flour. Warm up one cup of water. In a bowl, add ⅓ of the warm water to flour. Use spoon to mix about halfway, then use your hands until it's all mixed.

Add a generous amount of flour to your work surface. Using a little bit of muscle now, roll, knead, & incorporate all of your flour to make your cavatelli dough. Dough should not be sticky but not floury. If you touch it, it should not stick to you. If you press into it with your thumb, it should leave a nice imprint.

Once you've reached the right consistency, roll dough into a long strip, like a 1 ½ inch 'baguette' shape. Then, cut this into four slices, each about 4 inches long.

Separate 1 piece from the other 3. Cover the other 3 with a small bowl so that they don't dry out. Lightly flour your hands & roll your 1 piece of dough into another long noodle-type shape, very skinny baguette, about 1 inch thick. Then, cut into 1 inch pieces.

Take a gnocchi board OR large fork, put one of your pieces at the top of the board/fork & take two fingers to roll it down the board to make cavatelli ridges in your piece of pasta dough. You should end up with a thick 1 inch piece of pasta with spirals all the way around.

And look at that, my friends. You've just made homemade cavatelli with only two ingredients!

POTATO GNOCCHI

INGREDIENTS

3 cups riced white potatoes   1 cup all-purpose flour
1 whole egg

DIRECTIONS

Bring a pot of salted water to a boil. Peel & boil your potatoes. Once cooked all the way through, put potatoes through a potato ricer. You'll need 3 cups of riced potatoes.

Then, mix all ingredients together to create your gnocchi dough. Use more flour if too sticky or more water if dough is too dry.

Flour your work surface & lightly wet your hands before working with your dough. Roll out dough into a long log shape. Cut into quarters.

Begin with your first quarter & roll into a long, skinny rope shape. Then, using a bench scraper, cut into 1 inch gnocchis.

Keep pushing around your gnocchis into the flour to keep them from sticking.

You are ready to boil your gnocchis! Place in boiling water & cook until al dente.

RICOTTA CAVATELLI

INGREDIENTS

1 whole egg
2 ½ cups all-purpose flour

1 cup ricotta cheese
½ cup warm water

DIRECTIONS

Bring a pot of salted water to a boil. Warm up ½ cup of warm water.

In a bowl, add egg & flour together and mix. You can use a fork. Then, add ricotta cheese & water. Mix with fork until it almost becomes a ball of pasta dough.

Sprinkle flour on your work surface. Wet your hands with a little warm water & add dough to your work surface. Knead until you get a nice, soft dough.

Now, roll into a very thick log & cut into four, 4 inch logs.

Next, roll each of the 4 inch logs into a thin 1 inch thick baguette shape. Cut again into small, 1-2 inch pieces.

Take one piece to a gnocchi board OR a big fork and roll backward with two fingers to create the cavatelli ridges.

Add all cavatellis to a floured dish & then boil for about 10-15 minutes, or until al dente.

Serve with your favorite sauce & enjoy!

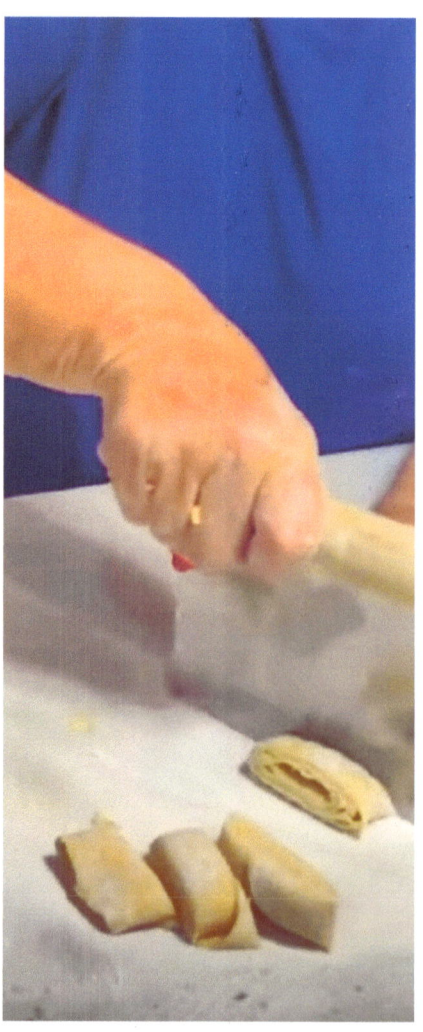

TAGLIATELLE
Using only two ingredients, let's make tagliatelle!

INGREDIENTS

3 whole eggs   2 cups all-purpose flour

DIRECTIONS

Sift all flour. Then, take your flour & make a wheel shape on your work surface. Now, add your eggs right into the center. Use your hands to mix. You want to make a soft dough, so use as much flour as you need but add in small increments.

Incorporate all flour completely into your dough. The final consistency should be soft but not sticky. You should be able to hold it with your hands without it sticking to you. And if you press down with your finger into the dough, it should leave a nice imprint.

Once you have your beautiful dough, let it sit, covered, for 10-15 minutes.

After, roll out your dough using a rolling pin & flatten entirely.

Next, time to run your pasta dough through a 'pasta maker' machine. Pass through twice. Now, on a floured work surface, with each long, flattened piece that you now have, cut right down the middle, short ways. Then, roll all of your halves. Then, chop each halve to make ½ inch to 1 inch ribbons. Unravel to see the beautiful tagliatelle that you made!

Notes
When you make pasta, you must have fun with it!

BUCATINI E CECI
bucatini with chickpeas

INGREDIENTS

1 lb bucatini pasta
1 can chickpeas
1 6oz can tomato paste
½ white onion

Parmigiano reggiano
OR pecorino romano
½ cup TUK Olive Oil
Pink salt & black pepper
Fresh herbs:
Basil

DIRECTIONS

Bring a pot of salted water to a boil & prepare a large, deep pan over medium heat. You can use fresh chickpeas, of course, but if using canned, wash & strain well. Chop white onion.

Cook your bucatini. Remove from heat once cooked al dente.

While you wait, let's make the sauce! Add oil to hot pan & sauté your white onion. Stir around until a little translucent. Then, add tomato paste. Mix until olive oil separates from tomato & onion. Then add pasta water, ¼ cup at a time, as needed, to thicken.

Once thickened, add your ceci beans into the sauce. Stir intermittently for about 10 minutes. Add pink salt, black pepper, & fresh basil.

When ready to plate, serve pasta first. Add ceci & sauce on top. Finish with olive oil, basil, & parmigiano reggiano or pecorino romano.

ESCAROLE & CANNELLINI BEANS

INGREDIENTS

Lots of escarole!
2 cloves fresh garlic
2 pepperoncinos
1 can cannellini beans

½ cup water
TUK Olive Oil

DIRECTIONS

Prepare a pan over medium heat. Chop escarole & garlic.

To a hot pan, coat with olive oil. Then, add garlic & pepperoncino. Once the garlic becomes aromatic, add your cannellini beans. Stir and season with pink salt & black pepper to taste.

Next, add your beautiful escarole to the pan. Add ½ cup water & cover your pan.

When escarole is softened, you are ready to plate & serve.

DANDELION PASTA

With angel hair, this dish is my favorite!

INGREDIENTS

1 lb angel hair pasta
Lots of dandelion!
1 white onion
3-4 pepperoncinos
1 carrot
1 cup cherry tomatoes
5 small mushrooms

3 cloves fresh garlic
Pink salt & black pepper
TUK Olive Oil
Fresh herbs:
Basil

DIRECTIONS

Bring a pot of salted water to a boil. Chop onion, carrot, tomato, mushroom, & garlic. Prepare a pan over medium heat.

To a hot pan, coat the bottom with olive oil. Sauté onion, carrot, mushroom, garlic, & pepperoncinos. Stir around for a few moments & season with pink salt & black pepper to your liking. Now, add your cherry tomatoes.

Add dandelion to your boiling water. Then, add angel hair pasta, too.

Once pasta & dandelion have softened, start adding a little pasta water at a time to your pan of veggies.

Now, plate! Add your pasta & dandelion to a dish. Then, cover with your beautiful veggies. Finish with fresh basil & a few more pepperoncinos...but only if you like it hot!

FETTUCINE GIALLE Y VERDE
yellow & green fettuccine

INGREDIENTS

½ lb spinach fettucine pasta
½ lb fettucine pasta
3 cups heavy whipping cream
½ stick salted butter
½ shallot
Zest of 1 lemon, thick rind

1-2 tsp ground nutmeg
½ cup parmigiano reggiano
Pink salt & black pepper
TUK Olive Oil

DIRECTIONS

Bring a pot of salted water to a boil & prepare a pan over medium heat. Dice your shallot.

Add oil to your hot pan. Add your shallot & sauté. Once sautéed, add 3 cups heavy whipping cream & parmigiano reggiano. Stay on medium heat. Add pink salt & black pepper to taste followed by ½ stick of salted butter. Let simmer.

Meanwhile, boil your pasta.

Sprinkle freshly grated or ground nutmeg to your pan for a beautiful flavor & add the zest of one whole lemon rind.

When pasta is cooked al dente, add to your pan & mix together.
Serve & finish with parmigiano reggiano.

Notes
The firmer and thicker the lemon and rind, the better!

HOT GARLIC PASTA

Hot, hot pasta using my hot, hot olive oil!

INGREDIENTS

1 lb pasta of your choice
1-3 pepperoncinos
1-2 cloves fresh garlic
A few plum tomatoes

½ cup parmigiano reggiano
TUK *Hot* Olive Oil
Pink salt & black pepper
Fresh herbs:
Basil

DIRECTIONS

Bring a pot of salted water to a boil. Prepare a pan over medium heat. Finely chop your tomatoes & garlic.

Add your pasta to the boiling water. Add TUK *Hot* Olive Oil to hot pan. When pan sizzles, add your red hot pepperoncinos & chopped garlic. Let sauté.

To your pan, add tomato, pink salt, & black pepper to taste. Sauté for a few minutes but do not burn the garlic. Turn down the heat if needed.

When pasta is done, strain & add to your hot olive oil pan. Add parmigiano reggiano, fresh basil, & give a final toss before serving. Garnish with more basil!

PASTA BROCCOLI

Sara's Way

INGREDIENTS

1 lb pasta of your choice
1 head of broccoli
A few stalks of celery
1 white onion
1 green onion

2-3 plum tomatoes
1 large carrot
TUK Olive Oil
Pink salt & black pepper
Fresh herbs:
Basil

DIRECTIONS

Bring a pot of salted water to a boil & prepare a pan over medium heat.

Finely chop tomato, carrot, white onion, & green onion. Finely chop celery, including the leafy part of the celery. Separate your raw broccoli into smaller florets. Add broccoli florets to boiling water.

Add ½ cup olive oil to hot pan. Once simmering, add all chopped ingredients, pink salt & black pepper. Let sauté.

Once the broccoli is cooked, remove the broccoli & set aside & then add your pasta to the same boiling water to cook. When the pasta is about halfway cooked, pour broccoli back into the pasta. At this time, add about 1/4 cup of pasta water to your sauté pan. Allow veggies to fully soften. Add more pasta water if needed.

Okay, we're ready to plate! Grab a large dish & then use tongs or a straining spoon to put all pasta & broccoli onto your dish. Then, pour your sautéed veggies over your pasta broccoli.

Add a little bit of the remaining veggie liquid from the pan over the top of the dish. Delicious! And last, drizzle all over with olive oil & add big, beautiful pieces of fresh basil.

Notes

This pasta broccoli should have a little liquid that falls to the bottom of the dish.

PASTA E FAGIOLI
pasta with beans

INGREDIENTS

½ lb penne pasta
1 can cannellini beans
2 cloves fresh garlic
¼ red onion
½ white onion
2 pepperoncinos

3 plum tomatoes
¾ 6oz can tomato paste
Parmigiano reggiano
TUK *Hot* Olive Oil
Pink salt & black pepper
Fresh herbs:
Basil

DIRECTIONS

Prepare a pan over medium heat. Bring a pot of salted water to a boil.
Chop your tomatoes, garlic, & onions. Keep all separate. Rinse & drain your cannellini beans.

Add a few tablespoons of olive oil to your hot pan. Add garlic, onions, & pepperoncinos. Let sauté until a little translucent. Then, add tomatoes, tomato paste, pink salt, & black pepper. Once the tomato starts to caramelize & stick to pan, add your cannellini beans & 1 cup of water. Lower the heat to a soft simmer & add fresh basil.

While that simmers on low heat, go ahead & boil your pasta. After the pasta cooks for a few minutes, add about ¼ cup at a time of pasta water, as needed to thicken, to your pan.

Strain pasta lightly & add directly to your pan. Gently mix. Then, you're ready to plate!

Grate some parmigiano reggiano on top & finish with a drizzle of TUK *Hot* Olive Oil & fresh basil leaves.

I hope you enjoy this Pasta e Fagioli, Sara's Way!

PASTA RAPINI

pasta with broccoli rabe

INGREDIENTS

1 lb spaghetti no 5
1 bundle rapini
3 cloves fresh garlic
Optional:
2-3 pepperoncinos

½ cup TUK Olive Oil
Pink salt & black pepper
½ cup parmigiano reggiano or pecorino romano

DIRECTIONS

Bring a pot of salted water to a boil & prepare a large pan over medium heat. Slice your rapini long ways. Chop your garlic.

To your hot pan, add your olive oil & sauté garlic and optional pepperoncinos. Once cooked, remove from heat.

Boil rapini. When half cooked, remove & add to your garlic & pepperoncinos. Now, cook your pasta by adding it into the same water as your rapini.

When done, pick up pasta with tongs & add to pan with rapini. Add back to a low heat for a low simmer. Sauté all together. Add pasta water as needed. This dish needs to be juicy!

While still in the pan, grate some parmigiano reggiano or pecorino romano on top & finish with a drizzle of fresh olive oil on top. Now, you are ready to plate!

A note for anchovy lovers

I love anchovies! So, when I sauté my garlic, I sauté about 2 or 3 anchovies, too. I love it! If you love anchovies, the flavor of this plate will amaze you.

SPAGHETTI CON FAGIOLINI VERDE
spaghetti with green beans

INGREDIENTS

1 lb spaghetti pasta
2 lb fresh green beans
3-4 plum tomatoes
1 small carrot
1 stalk of celery

3 cloves fresh garlic
1 pepperoncino
TUK Olive Oil
Pink salt & black pepper
Fresh herbs:
Basil

DIRECTIONS

Bring a pot of salted water to a boil. Chop garlic, tomato, celery, & carrot. Prepare a pan over medium heat.

Add green beans & spaghetti to boiling water together. Add olive oil to hot pan & sauté garlic, tomato, celery, carrot, & pepperoncino. Once fully sautéed, turn on very low heat to keep warm.

When pasta & green beans are done cooking, remove pasta & plate. I prefer my green beans a little tender so cook them to your own liking.

At this time, add about ¼ cup of pasta water to your sauté to thicken. When the consistency is to your liking, finish with pink salt & black pepper to taste. Pour on top of your spaghetti, add your green beans on top, & garnish with beautiful fresh basil.

TROFIE WITH CARCIOFI
trofie pasta with artichokes

INGREDIENTS

1 lb trofie pasta
1 can artichoke hearts
3 plum tomatoes
1 zucchini
½ white onion
2-3 tbsp capers

TUK Olive Oil
Provolone cheese
Pink salt & black pepper
Fresh herbs:
Basil

DIRECTIONS

Bring a pot of salted water to a boil. Chop your onion & tomatoes. Quarter your artichoke hearts. Very thinly shave your zucchini. Prepare a pan over medium heat.

To your hot pan, add a little olive oil. Then, add white onion. Once translucent, add tomato, basil, pink salt, & black pepper.

When tomato is almost done cooking, add your shaved zucchini & trofie pasta to your pot of boiling water. Add your artichoke hearts to your hot pan. Simmer on low-medium heat while your pasta & zucchini finish cooking together.

When the pasta & zucchini are ready, strain & add to the veggie pan. Add a few tbsp of pasta water to the pan to thicken if needed. Taste! Add more pink salt or black pepper if you need. Finish beautifully with capers, mix in, and let cook on low for a few moments.

Plate to a large dish. Serve & grate fresh provolone on top.

STUFFED PORTOBELLO MUSHROOMS

INGREDIENTS

4 portobello mushrooms
1 clove fresh garlic
1 cup breadcrumbs
Marinara Sauce

Fresh mozzarella
Fresh provolone
Pecorino romano or parmigiano reggiano
TUK Olive Oil
Fresh herbs:
Basil
Italian parsley

DIRECTIONS

Preheat your oven to 350F. Wash your portobello mushrooms & prepare them on a baking sheet to be filled! Chop garlic & about 1 cup of parsley.

In a bowl, put 3 tbsp breadcrumbs, add half of your parsley, all garlic, & 2 tbsp olive oil.
In a second bowl, add the rest of your breadcrumbs & the remaining parsley.
In a third bowl, combine about 1 cup marinara sauce with a little parmigiano reggiano or pecorino romano.

Add a slice of provolone to the top of the mushroom. Then, add garlic parsley mixture. Add a few small spoonfuls of marinara followed by fresh slices of mozzarella. Take one full leaf of basil & tuck it just underneath one of the slices of mozzarella. Then, more marinara on top. Last, add the breadcrumb parsley mixture, & finish with pecorino romano or parmigiano reggiano. Follow these steps for all of your mushrooms. Don't waste any ingredients, add any remaining ingredients to your liking!

Bake at 350F for about 15-20 minutes or until softened & with a bubbly top!

MUSHROOM ASPARAGUS RISOTTO

INGREDIENTS

2 cups uncooked risotto rice
1 container small mushrooms
½ bundle asparagus
3 green onions
1 plum tomato
Broth: chicken/beef or veggie

½ stick salted butter
Parmigiano reggiano
TUK Olive Oil
Pink salt & black pepper
Optional:
Whole peppercorns

DIRECTIONS

Prepare a large pan over medium heat. Chop green onions, tomatoes, mushrooms, & asparagus. Place 3-4 cups of broth, store-bought or homemade, in a saucepan & leave warm.

To your hot pan, add salted butter. Sauté your tomato & green onions. Once aromatic & a little translucent, add asparagus & mushrooms. Season generously with pink salt & black pepper. Allow your veggies to simmer for about 10 minutes. Add more oil if needed.

After about 10 minutes, add your uncooked risotto to your pan. Stir gently for a few moments. At this time, begin adding broth to your pan in half cup increments. Start with a few pours. Simmer should begin to slow, just keep stirring in your broth.

It should take roughly 20 minutes from the time you add your uncooked risotto to plating time. So, if all liquid is gone before the risotto is fully cooked, just keep adding more broth in small increments until risotto is fully cooked. In addition, add a small slice of butter every now & then. Taste test frequently until you reach your desired level of creaminess.

All done? Add some freshly grated parmigiano reggiano to the pan & mix before removing from heat, for an extra smooth texture. Add as much as you'd like. At this time, feel free to add some whole peppercorns. That's what I like to do. Also, if you feel your risotto is still too dry, keep adding broth until you feel good about it!

Plate & top with more parmigiano reggiano. Enjoy this deliciously creamy risotto!

CASARECCE CON PISELLI, POMODORI, E PANCETTA

casarecce pasta with green peas, tomatoes, & pancetta

INGREDIENTS

1 lb casarecce pasta
¼ red onion
1 cup cherry tomatoes
2 cups green peas, frozen

3 pepperoncinos
1 cup pancetta
TUK Olive Oil

DIRECTIONS

Bring a pot of salted water to a boil & prepare a pan over low-medium heat. Chop red onion. Chop pancetta if needed. Keep separate.

Cook your pasta.
Add olive oil to your hot pan. Once hot, add red onion, pancetta, pepperoncinos, whole cherry tomatoes, & frozen green peas. Let sauté on a low-medium heat.

Once pasta is al dente, plate onto a large dish. Add ¼ cup at a time of pasta water to your hot sauté pan to prepare your sauce to the consistency of your liking.

When ready, pour over your pasta & enjoy!

ZUCCHINI MEATBALLS

INGREDIENTS

2 whole eggs
½ Italian bread, few days old
2 cups grated zucchini
¼ cup parmigiano reggiano
¼ cup pecorino romano

2 cloves fresh garlic
TUK Dried Spices
TUK Olive Oil
Pink salt & black pepper
Fresh herbs:
Italian parsley

DIRECTIONS

Grate your zucchini to yield about 2 cups. Drain with your hands & put in large mixing bowl. Finely chop your garlic & about 1/2 cup parsley. Shred about 1-2 cups of Italian bread with the crust, blend in a blender to make 1 cup of breadcrumbs. Then, add to a mixing bowl with grated zucchini. Add 1 teaspoon dried spices. Add pink salt, black pepper, garlic, & parsley. Add two eggs, parmigiano reggiano, & pecorino romano.

Blend all together with your hands. Add more breadcrumbs, parmigiano reggiano, and/or pecorino romano, if needed, if your mixture is too wet. The firmer your mixture, the better.

Make your meatballs & place onto a dish. You'll want to cook them all at the same time so prepare them all first before cooking.

Prepare a pan over medium-high heat. Once hot, coat the bottom in a thick layer of olive oil. When ready to fry, add meatballs, a few at a time without touching. Fry all the way around until a thorough golden brown. Plate onto a bed of paper towels first to absorb the excess oil.

Then, serve & enjoy!

LASAGNA BOLOGNESE
To my husband & my son. Dedicated to you for every birthday.

INGREDIENTS

1 lb lasagna noodles, packaged OR freshly homemade
4 lbs ground beef
2 lbs ground pork
6 large carrots
1 bundle celery
2-3 white onions
Béchamel Sauce
Fresh Marinara Sauce

2 6oz cans tomato paste
1 jar tomato puree
1 cup white wine
1 cup parmigiano reggiano
1 cup TUK Olive Oil
3 tbsp ground nutmeg
Pink salt & black pepper

DIRECTIONS

Notes

For this Lasagna Bolognese, I would encourage you to use the homemade Tagliatelle recipe earlier in this section, 'Primo,' for your lasagna noodles. Cut the length of your noodles to the length of your lasagna baking dish & keep each of them about 4 inches wide.

Prepare two large 8qt pots over low-medium heat. Finely mince carrot, celery, & white onion. You'll need 3 cups of each. If you are using fresh nutmeg, go ahead and grate & set aside. To one of your hot pots, coat the bottom lightly in olive oil. Sauté all meat together. Only sauté until the meat is not red anymore. Then, remove & drain all liquid using a colander. Set meat aside for now.

To your other hot pot, add 1 cup olive oil. Now, sauté onion, celery, & carrot. Once veggies have softened, add all of your cooked meat into this pot, pink salt, & black pepper. Add 1 cup white wine. Let evaporate for about 5 minutes. Mix all together gently. Now, add all tomato paste & tomato puree. Cook for 5 more minutes. Add two cups of water. Turn the heat down and cook on a low simmer for 3-4 hours, uncovered. This is now your meat sauce! Check in to stir every once in a while. In the meantime, if you don't have any pre-prepared, make your béchamel & fresh marinara sauces. Both recipes can be found in the "Sugo" section of this book.

Once your sauce has reached a nice, thick consistency, it's time to preheat the oven to 350F.

If using packaged noodles, follow the package instructions to prepare for assembly of your lasagna. If using the Tagliatelle recipe in this book, bring some salted water to a boil & boil for just a few moments & then remove.

Now, time to assemble! First, coat the bottom of your baking dish with marinara sauce. Then, lay your first layer of lasagna noodles. Then, a layer of meat sauce. Don't skimp! Then, add a layer of parmigiano reggiano. Next, a layer of béchamel sauce. This completes your first layer! Start your second layer with a few spoonfuls of marinara, meat sauce, parmigiano reggiano, & béchamel -- in that order. Repeat for about 2-3 layers. Finish off your top layer with béchamel & parmigiano reggiano.

Bake at 350F for at least 30 minutes. Once the top is crispy & you can see the layers boiling, it's ready! But first, let your lasagna rest for at least 30 minutes before cutting into it. The lasagna bolognese must be perfect!

MANICOTTI

This is my elite, 'haute couture' designer recipe!

INGREDIENTS

8 whole eggs
2 cups all-purpose flour
¼ cup TUK Olive Oil
2 cups water

Béchamel Sauce
Marinara Sauce
Salted, softened butter

Yield: 24 crepes

DIRECTIONS

Prepare a pan over low-medium heat. You need to make your crepes first.

Mix your eggs with the flour. Beat with an electric hand mixer or blender, until batter looks like pancake batter. Add water if it's too thick. This batter should fall through a fork, not stick to it. Add water until you reach this consistency.

Brush your hot pan with olive oil completely. You are now ready to fry your crepes! Use a ⅓ measuring cup to make your crepes so that each turns out the same size. Now, remember, the first crepe you make is always going to be bad! It will be okay after that. Leave heat on the exact same level throughout cooking of all crepes. Re-brush the pan with olive oil after every third crepe or more frequently if needed.

So, fill your ⅓ cup with batter & pour into pan slowly. Tip the pan around to fill the bottom of the pan with a thin layer of crepe batter. Cook about 1 minute each side. If you can, lift with your fingers & flip, or you can use a fork or spatula. Remove each crepe from pan & start creating a stack of them. Once you have your completed stack of beautiful lightly brown spotted crepes, it's time to make your manicotti filling.

Proceed to the next page for next steps.

Notes
I like to make extra crepes & freeze them! If you also decide to freeze them, lay them flat.

MANICOTTI FILLING

First, here are two meatless options for your ricotta filling.

INGREDIENTS

Manicotti with Ricotta
1 whole egg
1 egg yolk
1 container ricotta cheese
1 container fresh mozzarella
1 cup parmigiano reggiano
Pink salt & black pepper

Manicotti with Ricotta & Spinach
1 whole egg
1 egg yolk
1-2 cups frozen spinach
1 container ricotta cheese
1 container fresh mozzarella
1 cup parmigiano reggiano
Pink salt & black pepper

DIRECTIONS

Manicotti with Ricotta

Drain ricotta of all water & place into a bowl. Beat 1 whole egg & 1 yolk in a separate bowl and add pink salt & black pepper. Now, you can add the ricotta into that bowl. Then, add all parmigiano reggiano & all of your fresh mozzarella. This mixture should not become runny if the ricotta was fully drained. This completes your 'manicotti stuffed with ricotta' mixture!

Manicotti with Ricotta & Spinach

Defrost frozen spinach & drain excess water completely. Drain ricotta of all water & place into a bowl. Beat 1 whole egg & 1 egg yolk in a separate bowl and add pink salt & black pepper. Now, you can add the ricotta into that bowl. Then, add all parmigiano reggiano, all of your fresh mozzarella, & spinach. This completes your 'manicotti stuffed with ricotta & spinach' mixture!

If you choose one of these options & are ready to fill your manicotti crepes, proceed:
Preheat your oven to 350F. Add a few spoonfuls of filling to your crepes & roll lightly. Now, brush the bottom of a large baking dish with softened salted butter. Add a few spoonfuls of béchamel sauce onto the bottom. Then, lay your stuffed manicotti crepes down on the dish. Pour more béchamel on top. Then, add a sprinkle of parmigiano reggiano. Finish with a layer of marinara sauce.

For both filling options, bake at 350F for 20 minutes or until the top is bubbly & brown.

CANNELLONI WITH PORK, VEAL, & BEEF

This recipe is to be used with the 'manicotti' crepes recipe.

INGREDIENTS

½ lb ground pork
½ lb ground veal
½ lb ground beef
½ white onion

TUK Olive Oil
Pink salt & black pepper
Bechamel Sauce
Marinara Sauce
Softened, salted butter

DIRECTIONS

Preheat your oven to 350F & prepare a large pan over medium heat. Dice white onion.

Once pan is hot, add a little olive oil & then add all of your meat & sauté together.

Once cooked, add your white onion & at least 2 cups of marinara sauce to the pan. Use more if you want more! Simmer on low-medium heat for about five minutes.

Add a few spoonfuls of filling to your crepes & roll lightly. Now, brush the bottom of a large baking dish with softened salted butter. Add a few spoonfuls of béchamel onto the bottom. Then, lay your stuffed crepes down on the dish. Pour more béchamel on top. Then, add a sprinkle of parmigiano reggiano. Finish with a layer of marinara sauce. Now, you have homemade cannelloni!

Bake at 350F for 20 minutes or until the top is bubbly & brown.

CANNELLONI WITH CHICKEN

This recipe is to be used with the 'manicotti' crepes recipe.

INGREDIENTS

2 chicken breasts
1 whole egg
1 egg yolk
1 stick softened salted butter
1 cup parmigiano reggiano

1 cup white wine
TUK Olive Oil
Pink salt & black pepper

DIRECTIONS

This particular recipe is to fill 12 crepes, which should feed about 6 people.

Preheat your oven to 350F & prepare a pan over medium heat.

To your hot pan, add a few tbsp of olive oil & 1/2 stick softened salted butter. Then, add your chicken breasts. Season with pink salt & black pepper. Turn over after about five minutes. Once chicken is almost cooked through, about 10-15 minutes total, add 1 cup of white wine. Cover & let simmer for about five minutes. Add a little water if needed.

Once chicken is fully cooked, remove from heat & ground the chicken using a blender.

Put ground chicken into a bowl. Add 1 cup parmigiano reggiano, your 1 whole egg & 1 egg yolk, pink salt, & black pepper. Mix together. This is now your chicken cannelloni mixture!

Add a few spoonfuls of filling to your crepes & roll lightly. Now, brush the bottom of a large baking dish with softened salted butter. Add a few spoonfuls of béchamel onto the bottom. Then, lay your cannellonis down on the dish. Pour more béchamel on top. Then, add a sprinkle of parmigiano reggiano. Finish with a layer of marinara sauce.

Bake at 350F for 20 minutes or until the top is bubbly & brown.

ORECHIETTE CON RAPINI Y SALCICCIA
orechiette pasta with broccoli rabe & sausage

INGREDIENTS

1 lb orecchiette pasta, pre-cooked
3-4 Italian sausage links
Lots of rapini!
½ red onion
¼ cup TUK Olive Oil

DIRECTIONS

Good orecchiette pasta takes about 45 minutes to cook. If you have the extra time, you can cook fresh orecchiette. But for this recipe, it is assumed that you have pre-cooked your orecchiette.

Bring a pot of salted water to a boil & prepare a large, deep pan over medium heat. Pre-cook the sausage in the hot pan with water only & then rinse. Cut up into any shape you like. Rough chop your red onion.

Add olive oil to your hot pan. Add sausage & onion.

To the boiling water, add lots and lots of rapini, turn down the heat to a softer boil & cover.

Keep stirring onion and sausage over medium heat. Should be a low simmer.

Pour your cooked orecchiette into the pot of rapini. Let them cook together for about five minutes. Salt to your liking but keep covered until ready to serve.

When ready to serve, add your orecchiette & rapini to the sausage & onion. Mix together gently on low heat & add olive oil generously.

Plate, serve, & enjoy!

A comment from G.S. on The Unexpected Kitchen's live show:
"Wish we had smellavision!"

RIGATONI AL FORNO
baked rigatoni

INGREDIENTS

1 lb rigatoni pasta
4 cups Marinara Sauce
2 cups meatballs
2 whole eggs
4 hard boiled eggs
TUK Olive Oil

1 cup parmigiano reggiano
1 container fresh mozzarella
¼ cup breadcrumbs
Fresh herbs:
Basil
Italian parsley

DIRECTIONS

Finely chop your parsley. If you don't already have 4 hard boiled eggs, make some! They need to be fresh & fully cooked. When your eggs are ready, peel & slice in half – short ways.

Bring a pot of salted water to a boil for your pasta. Cook your pasta. *Pasta should be cooked no further than al dente because it will cook again in the oven later.*

Prepare a pan over medium heat. Once hot, add a few tablespoons of olive oil.
Add 2 cups small dime-sized or quarter-sized meatballs. You need to keep their shape so don't move them too much.

Preheat your oven 350F & prepare a baking dish, at least 2-3 inches deep. Add 2-3 big scoops of marinara to cover the bottom of the dish. Add drained rigatoni followed by a layer of shredded mozzarella. Add a few slices of hard-boiled eggs & a layer of meatballs. Finish this layer with parmigiano reggiano & more marinara sauce. Repeat this series of steps for your layers until your pan is full.

Add the last of your hard-boiled egg slices, 1/4 cup breadcrumbs, parmigiano reggiano, & more parsley. Then, whisk your two whole eggs & pour over the top of your dish. Add 2-3 tablespoons of water, pink salt, black pepper, & a little more marinara sauce.

Bake in the oven at 350F for 40-45 minutes or until the top is crispy to the touch!

LINGUINI WITH CLAMS

INGREDIENTS

1 lb linguini pasta
1 full container white clams
12 shelled clams
3 plum tomato, very ripe
4 cloves fresh garlic
1 small shallot

1 cup white wine
½ cup TUK Olive Oil
Fresh herbs:
Italian parsley

DIRECTIONS

Prepare a pan over medium heat. Finely mince your garlic, shallot, & parsley. Chop your tomatoes.

To a hot pan, add olive oil. Sauté garlic & shallot for a few moments. Pour in the container of clams. Cook for about 3 minutes. Add wine & allow to evaporate for a few minutes. Then, add tomatoes. Reduce heat & cover for a slow slimmer, about 10 minutes.

In the meantime, bring a pot of salted water to a boil.

After 10 minutes, add the shelled clams & parsley. Mix around gently. Once the clams open; they're done! Remove from heat about a minute later.

Boil your linguini. Add a little pasta water to your pan & mix in. Once linguini is cooked al dente, drain & plate on a platter. Pour all clams & sauce on top.

Decorate your plate with full strings of parsley.

LOBSTER FRA DIAVOLO

INGREDIENTS

1 lb spaghetti pasta
6 small lobsters
3-4 pepperoncinos
Fresh Marinara Sauce

Crushed red pepper flakes
TUK Olive Oil
Fresh herbs:
Basil

DIRECTIONS

For this recipe, you will need to make my fresh marinara sauce, not the 10-minute marinara sauce, which can be found in the "Sugo" section of this book.

So, the first step, if you haven't already, is to prepare the fresh marinara sauce.

Once prepared & simmered for a full two hours, add your lobsters directly to the marinara sauce. Add lots of crushed red pepper flakes & pepperoncinos. Let lobsters rest & marinate in that beautiful sauce for 15 minutes.

Meanwhile, cook your spaghetti in salted boiling water until cooked al dente.

When ready to plate, drain & serve spaghetti on a platter and place lobster & sauce on top. Finish with fresh basil & a drizzle of olive oil.

ROSEMARY PORK TENDERLOIN

INGREDIENTS

2 pork tenderloins
3-4 cloves fresh garlic

TUK Dried Spices
TUK Olive Oil
Pink salt & black pepper
Fresh herbs:
Rosemary

DIRECTIONS

Prepare a large pan over medium heat. Chop your garlic. Chop up a little rosemary but make sure you save plenty of full rosemary leaves.

First, coat your pork tenderloins in olive oil. Then, drench in delicious dried spices. Remember, when coating with the dried spices, use generously! It will be so flavorful.

To a hot pan, coat the bottom with olive oil. Sauté your garlic. Then, add 2 or 3 full leaves of fresh rosemary. Add your pork tenderloins directly on top of the rosemary leaves. Top with pink salt. Cover.

Turn over after about 3 minutes. Then, don't forget to cook the sides! Keep covered always.

When pork is done, let it rest on a plate with a cover on it. We want a soft, juicy, pink center, guys!

When ready to plate, cut into 2-inch thick slices & season with pink salt & black pepper. Serve on a large platter & clean it up a little bit. Present your pork tenderloin elegantly. Surround with fresh rosemary & herbs. This is a beautiful dish & I hope you enjoy.

Notes
Serve with sautéed spinach & boiled potatoes.

COTOLETTE
CUTLETS ... three ways!

INGREDIENTS

2 chicken breasts
3 whole eggs
2 cloves fresh garlic
1 cup all-purpose flour
1 cup breadcrumbs
Juice of 1 lemon

1 cup parmigiano reggiano
TUK Dried Spices
¼ cup TUK Olive Oil
¼ cup canola oil
Pink salt & black pepper
Fresh herbs:
Italian parsley

DIRECTIONS

First, flatten the chicken breasts. Finely chop garlic & parsley.

Make three bowls with the following: a first mixture of flour & parmigiano reggiano. Make a second mixture, combining your eggs with the lemon juice, garlic, parsley, pink salt, & black pepper. In the third bowl, add about 1 cup of breadcrumbs to start with.

Prepare a frying pan over medium-high heat. Once hot, add olive & canola oils.

You are ready to coat & fry your chicken. Sprinkle chicken thoroughly with pink salt, black pepper, & dried spices. Then, add flattened chicken breasts to flour & parmigiano reggiano mixture, then egg mixture, then coat generously with just breadcrumbs. Add to frying pan, turning over after about 3-5 minutes.

Once you've fried all of your chicken cutlets, allow to rest on bed of paper towels to absorb excess oil. When you're ready to plate, serve with lemon wedges & fresh Italian parsley.

Notes
You can use this recipe three ways! Chicken, pork, or beef.
Make sure you try them all!

I dedicate this recipe to my sister, Melina.
Every time I make this recipe, I think of her!

CRISPY CHICKEN THIGHS

INGREDIENTS

6-8 bone-in chicken thighs
3 cloves fresh garlic
1 cup white wine

TUK Olive Oil
Pink salt & black pepper
Fresh herbs:
Oregano
Rosemary

DIRECTIONS

Notes

For this recipe, I highly recommend that you soak your chicken thighs in water & white vinegar for two hours for maximum flavor.

Prepare a large pan over medium heat. Chop your garlic. If using fresh herbs, chop some of your oregano & rosemary.

To a hot pan, coat bottom in olive oil. Add your chicken thighs. Add pink salt, garlic, oregano, & rosemary to the pan. Toss every few minutes. Flip chicken thighs, add 1 cup white wine, & cover. Let simmer for about 10 minutes.

Time to plate! Top with fresh oregano & rosemary and enjoy.

STUFFED POLPETTONE

INGREDIENTS

1 lb ground, lean pork
1 lb ground sirloin
2 Italian sausage links
2 whole eggs
4 hard boiled eggs
2 cloves fresh garlic
¼ red onion
⅓ cup breadcrumbs
½ cup parmigiano reggiano
Fresh provolone

TUK Dried Spices
⅓ cup TUK Olive Oil
Marinara
Pink salt & black pepper
Fresh herbs:
Chive
Italian parsley
Rosemary
Sage

DIRECTIONS

Preheat your oven to 475F, prepare a pan over medium heat, & bring a pot of salted water to a boil. Finely chop your garlic & all fresh herbs. Leave some herbs whole. Chop your red onion.

To your hot pan, add a little olive oil. Then, add your Italian sausage & chopped red onion. Once sausage has cooked throughout, remove sausage & onion from pan. Then, mince this mixture to create a 'crumble' consistency. Set aside for later. To your boiling water, add 4 eggs to make your 4 hard boiled eggs. Peel once fully cooked.

Combine pork & sirloin in a large mixing bowl with your 2 raw eggs. Add about half of your garlic, a little parmigiano reggiano, pink salt, black pepper, all chopped fresh herbs, & a splash of dried spices. Combine & mix with a fork. Once thoroughly mixed, add breadcrumbs. Now, use your hands to combine. Add more breadcrumbs if needed but only add in small quantities at a time.

Transfer mixture to a large sheetpan lined with parchment paper. Flatten and stretch into a 1 inch thickness. Top with more parsley & parmigiano reggiano. Next, sprinkle the Italian sausage & red onion crumbles. Add large strips of provolone. Slice your hard boiled eggs in halves & lay right down the middle, from top to bottom.

Continued on next page.

STUFFED POLPETTONE

DIRECTIONS

Now, flatten this mixture completely by pressing down throughout. Grab the parchment paper underneath & use it to pull the mixture forward into a rolling motion. Roll tightly until you form a complete log shape. Dispose of parchment paper.

Now, coat the bottom of a glass baking dish with olive oil. Make a bed of beautiful herbs, using chive, parsley, rosemary, & sage. Make it beautiful! Then, add your polpettone to the middle of the dish, right on top of your herbs. Double check your polpettone, making sure it is clean & sealed. Lastly, please decorate your polpettone. Use more herbs! Add a drizzle of olive oil, a sprinkle of dried spices, & finish with grated parmigiano reggiano.

Add a few tablespoons of marinara to fully coat the surface of your polpettone.

Bake at 350F for 35 minutes.

SAUSAGE & PEPPERS

INGREDIENTS

6 sweet Italian sausage links
½ red onion
½ white onion
10 sweet baby peppers
3 cloves fresh garlic

Balsamic vinegar
Fresh herbs:
Oregano
Rosemary

DIRECTIONS

Bring a pot of water to a boil. While you wait, chop your onions in long slices. Remove all seeds from the peppers & cut in long slices, too.

To your boiling water, pre-boil your sausage links. Once they brown just a little, pierce the top of each with a knife. Let them continue to brown. You'll begin to notice the fat from the sausage rise to the water line.

Prepare a pan over medium heat. Chop up some fresh oregano, rosemary, & your garlic.

Coat the bottom of your hot pan with olive oil. Sauté your onions & garlic.

When the sausages are all the way brown on the outside, add directly on top of your onions & garlic. After, you'll add your sliced peppers. Move around gently & let everything cook together for a few minutes.

Once sausages begin to sear, remove just the sausages from the pan & slice how you'd like. Add them back to the pan followed by your chopped oregano & rosemary. Now, for the secret ingredient, add 1/4 cup of balsamic vinegar. Continue to cook for a few more minutes.

Ready to plate? Display sausage & peppers on a large platter and decorate with more oregano & rosemary. Delicious!

VEAL LIVER
This one is dedicated to Dan! It's his favorite.

INGREDIENTS

1 lb veal liver
½ white onion
½ red onion
Balsamic vinegar

TUK Olive Oil
Pink salt & black pepper
Fresh herbs:
Rosemary
Sage

DIRECTIONS

Notes

The reason why people like my veal liver is because first, I wash it with white vinegar!

So, wash your veal with 1 cup of white vinegar & then prepare a pan over medium heat.

Chop your red & white onion in long slices.

To your hot pan, coat the bottom in olive oil. Sauté your onions. When onions are about halfway cooked through, add your veal right on top of the onions. Season with pink salt & black pepper. Decorate your veal with full stalks of rosemary & full leaves of sage.

When the veal begins to bleed a little, it's time to flip and cook the other side. Each side should cook for about three minutes.

After the other side has seared, finish by adding 1/4 cup balsamic vinegar to the pan.

Easy, amazing veal liver. Plate, garnish with rosemary, and enjoy.

Let's make sardines! So simple!

First, clean out your sardines. Keep the heads if you want. Lightly coat in flour & fry in canola oil mixed with olive oil. Place on paper towels to absorb the excess oil. When ready to enjoy, plate and squeeze fresh lemon on top. Finish with large sprigs of fennel.

HERB CRUSTED SALMON

INGREDIENTS

6oz salmon fillet
Juice of ½ lemon
3 hearts of romaine
2 cloves fresh garlic

TUK Dried Spices
TUK Olive Oil
Pink salt & black pepper

DIRECTIONS

Prepare a pan over medium-high heat. On a plate, drizzle 1 teaspoon of olive oil over your beautiful piece of salmon. Then, coat with 3 tbsp of dried spices & a little pink salt. Use your hands to incorporate the dried spices, pink salt, & olive oil into the salmon to create a nice crispy coating. Then, chop your garlic.

To a hot pan, coat in olive oil. Sauté your garlic for just a moment & then add your salmon, skin side down.

After a minute or two, juice a little lemon directly on top of salmon.

Turn over after two minutes. Add more lemon juice on top of salmon.

Once fully cooked through & a very pale pink, time to plate.

Plate your salmon on a bed of romaine hearts & cover with your sautéed garlic. Add a drizzle of olive oil to finish.

STUFFED CALAMARI

INGREDIENTS

4-6 fresh calamari
3 cloves fresh garlic
½ Italian bread, few days old
¼ cup white wine

¼ cup parmigiano reggiano
TUK Olive Oil
Pink salt & black pepper
Fresh herbs:
Italian parsley

DIRECTIONS

Clean calamaris, take insides out, and chop tentacles into very fine tiny pieces to be used in stuffing later.

Blend your bread, including the crust, to create your breadcrumbs. Then, chop garlic & parsley. Add garlic, parsley, 1 cup breadcrumbs, parmigiano reggiano, 1/4 cup white wine, pink salt, & black pepper to a mixing bowl. Mix all together. This should make a loose mixture.

Now, take a spoon & stuff your calamaris.

Finish by sealing each calamari with a toothpick.

Now, it's time to choose your delicious sauce on the next page to go with your calamaris.

CALAMARI SAUCE
Now, choose a sauce to bake with your fresh, stuffed calamaris.

INGREDIENTS

Red Sauce
½ white onion
2 cloves fresh garlic
6 plum tomatoes
¼ cup TUK Olive Oil
Pink salt & black pepper
Fresh herbs:
Italian parsley

White Sauce
½ red onion
1 ½ cups white wine
¼ cup TUK Olive Oil
Pink salt & black pepper
Fresh herbs:
Italian parsley
Oregano
Rosemary
Thyme

DIRECTIONS

Red Sauce

Prepare a pan over medium heat. Remove all seeds & juices from tomatoes. Chop your tomatoes. Chop your onion, garlic, & parsley. To a hot pan, add olive oil. Then, sauté your onion & garlic. Once aromatic & a little translucent, add all of your tomatoes. Stir gently for a few moments. Add your stuffed calamaris on top of the red sauce. Add pink salt & black pepper to taste. Then, add parsley. Simmer for about 10-15 minutes. Plate, garnish with more parsley, & enjoy!

White Sauce

Preheat oven to 350F. Finely shave your red onion. Chop all herbs. To a glass baking dish, add ¼ cup olive oil, followed by shaved onion. Then, pour 1 cup white wine & 1 cup of mixed herbs. Add pink salt & black pepper to taste. Now, place your stuffed calamaris on top. Pour a little more white wine over the top. Bake at 350F for 35 minutes. Once out of the oven, garnish with any remaining mixed herbs & serve. Delicious!

SUGO

AGLIO E OLIO
garlic & oil

INGREDIENTS

8-10 cloves fresh garlic
½ cup TUK Olive Oil

3 pepperoncinos
Pecorino romano or parmigiano reggiano

DIRECTIONS

Prepare a pan over low-medium heat. Thinly slice your garlic.

To your hot pan, add olive oil, then garlic & pepperoncinos. Sauté until garlic has softened.

If making for pasta, add your pasta, cooked al dente, directly to your aglio e olio. Plate & finish with fresh, shaved parmigiano reggiano or pecorino romano.

Notes
8-10 cloves of fresh garlic should be used per 1 lb of pasta.

AGLIO OLIO CON LE SARDE
garlic & oil with sardines

INGREDIENTS

8-10 cloves fresh garlic
½ cup TUK Olive Oil
3 pepperoncinos
Pecorino romano or
parmigiano reggiano

6-8 filleted sardines
Fresh herbs:
Basil or Oregano
Optional:
A handful of cherry tomatoes

DIRECTIONS

Prepare a pan over low-medium heat. Thinly slice your garlic.

To your hot pan, add olive oil, then garlic & pepperoncinos. Sauté until garlic has softened.

Once garlic has softened, add sardines & mix in. Last, add chopped, fresh basil or chopped, fresh oregano. Add cherry tomatoes if you'd like.

If making for pasta, add your pasta, cooked al dente, directly to your aglio olio con le sarde.

Plate & finish with fresh, shaved parmigiano reggiano or pecorino romano.

10-MINUTE MARINARA

INGREDIENTS

½ white onion
½ small can tomato paste
1 can diced tomatoes

¼ cup TUK Olive Oil
Pink salt & black pepper
Fresh herbs:
Basil

DIRECTIONS

Prepare a large saucepan over medium heat. Add diced tomatoes to a blender to turn into a puree.

Then, chop your onion. I prefer a large chop for marinara, but you can do what you like. Add olive oil to hot saucepan. Add onion & sauté for a few minutes.

Next, add tomato paste, pink salt, & black pepper. Continue to sauté.

Once the oil starts to separate from the tomato & onion, it's time to pour the tomato puree. Then, reduce your heat to a low simmer & cook for about 10 more minutes.

After, add some beatiful fresh basil to the pot.

Now, your very own marinara sauce is ready...in only ten minutes!

FRESH MARINARA

INGREDIENTS

1 white onion
1 6oz can tomato paste
8-10 plum tomatoes, overly ripe
3 cloves fresh garlic

TUK Olive Oil
Pink salt & black pepper

DIRECTIONS

Prepare a large 6q pot over medium heat. Chop garlic & onion.

Next, you need to puree your plum tomatoes. But first, cut them & remove all seeds & liquid. Then, add to a blender to create your tomato puree.

To your hot pot, coat the bottom with at least 1 cup of olive oil.
Start by sauteing your onion & garlic with all of the tomato paste. Once it begins to thicken, add tomato puree. Lower the heat to a simmer, add pink salt & black pepper, cover, & let simmer for 2 hours.

There you have it, my friends. Sara's Fresh Marinara! Use with so many different recipes in this book! Please enjoy.

PESTO

INGREDIENTS

4 cups fresh basil
½ cup pine nuts
6 cloves fresh garlic

1 cup TUK Olive Oil
1 cup parmigiano reggiano
Pink salt & black pepper

DIRECTIONS

Wash & dry your fresh basil. Grate your parmigiano reggiano.

Peel your garlic. Add oil & garlic to a blender. Then, slowly add basil, little by little. The final step is to add the pine nuts & parmigiano reggiano. Add a little pink salt & black pepper.

Notes
Typically, 1 lb of pasta should need at least ½ cup of pesto.
Garlic should be really fresh which means it should not be turning yellow.
I love to grind black peppercorns for my pesto.
Have extra pesto? Just freeze it! Don't waste!

SPINACH JALAPEÑO PESTO

INGREDIENTS

4 cups fresh spinach
4 green onions
1 green jalapeño

3 cloves fresh garlic
½ cup pine nuts
1 cup parmigiano reggiano
¼ cup TUK Olive Oil

DIRECTIONS

Bring a pot of salted water to a boil. Just enough water to cover spinach in a moment. Chop green onion, separating whites from greens. You'll only use the whites, so you can save the greens for later use or garnish your pasta with a few! Cut your garlic & jalapeño.

Add spinach to boiling water to cook.

Once cooked, add spinach to a blender with your olive oil & whites of the green onion. Then, add garlic, jalapeño, pine nuts, & parmigiano reggiano.

Blend!

Mix your homemade spinach jalapeño pesto into your favorite pasta.

BÉCHAMEL

INGREDIENTS

1 stick salted butter
6 cups whole milk
4 tbsp all-purpose flour

1 tsp ground nutmeg
Pink salt & white pepper, not black!

DIRECTIONS

Prepare a large, deep saucepan over low-medium heat. Warm up your milk separately, either in another pan or a microwave.

To your hot saucepan, add butter & melt.

Once melted, add your flour to the butter & mix gently until it forms a paste. Move the pan off the burner & add milk very slowly. Once all milk has been added, you can move your pan back to the heat. Keep stirring. Add nutmeg, pink salt, & white pepper.

If béchamel becomes too thick, remove from burner again & add more warm milk while stirring.

Cook for a few minutes to your desired consistency. Then, give it a taste test! Add more pink salt & white pepper to your liking.

MY FATHER'S SUNDAY SAUCE
Cin cin, Papa!

INGREDIENTS

1 pork loin
3 italian sausage
2 chicken breast
1 can tomato paste
4 cups crushed tomatoes
1 white onion
3 cloves fresh garlic

1 cup TUK Olive Oil
TUK Dried Spices
Pink salt & black pepper
Fresh herbs:
Basil
Italian parsley

DIRECTIONS

Prepare two large, deep pans over medium heat. Chop fresh garlic, parsley, & onion. Keep onion separate. Wash chicken & pork with white vinegar & pat dry.

To the pork loin & chicken, cut 1-inch slits, each about 2 inches deep. Stuff half of the garlic & parsley into these slits.

Add ½ cup olive oil to each hot pan. In the first pan, add sausage & onion. To the second pan, add your pork loin. Season with pink salt & pepper.

Sauté sausage & onion for a few moments & then add tomato paste.

Turn pork loin over to roast the other side. Once pork has roasted on both sides, add pork to the sausage & onion. To the same pan used to cook the pork loin, add chicken & season with dried spices, pink salt, & black pepper.

Add crushed tomatoes & pink salt to your pan with the sausage, onion, & pork loin.

When ready, turn chicken over & season with dried spices, pink salt, & black pepper. Once about 70% cooked, add chicken breasts, slits facing up, to the other pan. Last, add your fresh basil.

Cook for one hour & serve with your favorite pasta.

CONTORNO

GARDEN CASSEROLE

INGREDIENTS

1 red onion
3 tomatoes
3 potatoes
1 zucchini, yellow or green
2 Japanese eggplant
Pink salt & black pepper

½ cup breadcrumbs
½ cup parmigiano reggiano
TUK Dried Spices
TUK Olive Oil
Fresh herbs:
Basil
Rosemary

DIRECTIONS

Prepare an oven-friendly pan, like a cast iron skillet & preheat your oven to 350F. Cut ¼ inch slices of zucchini, eggplant, tomato, onion, & potato – all same size & shape. In a bowl, mix ½ cup breadcrumbs with ½ cup parmigiano reggiano.

Coat the bottom of your pan with about 2-3 tablespoons of olive oil. Layer veggies around the pan, making it beautiful any way you like. Sprinkle all over with pink salt, black pepper, & dried spices. Add leaves of fresh basil…the more the better. Don't be skimpy! Sprinkle sprigs of fresh rosemary. Drizzle delicious olive oil on top. Last, add parmigiano reggiano & breadcrumb mixture all over.

Bake in the oven at 350F for 40-45 minutes or until you get a beautiful crispy top.

*A beautiful variety of broccoli & cauliflower florets.
Blanched then dressed in TUK Dressing & heirloom cherry tomatoes.*

ROASTED BRUSSELS SPROUTS
with rosemary & parmigiano reggiano

INGREDIENTS

1 bundle raw brussels sprouts
½ cup parmigiano reggiano
½ cup breadcrumbs

TUK Olive Oil
TUK Dried Spices
Fresh herbs:
Rosemary

DIRECTIONS

Preheat your oven to 450F.

Bring a pot of water to a boil. Slice brussels sprouts evenly in halves. Chop a bundle of fresh rosemary & set aside. Mix breadcrumbs with parmigiano reggiano in a small bowl & set aside.

Steam brussels sprouts. Coat the bottom of any baking dish with olive oil. Then, sprinkle 3-4 big spoonfuls of TUK Dried Spices on top of the olive oil. Finally, sprinkle ½ cup parmigiano reggiano & breadcrumb mixture.

When brussels sprouts are just about fully steamed, place one layer of halved brussels sprouts flat face down right onto the spices. Top with fresh rosemary followed by breadcrumb & parmigiano reggiano mixture. This dish is only one layer of brussels sprouts, each sprout super-packed with flavor!

Bake at 450F for 10-15 minutes or until crispy & browned on top. Mmmm, amazing!

Sometimes, it's all in how you present the most simple ingredients. Here is one of my favorites. Fresh green beans, yellow & green zucchini squash, & delicate asparagus. I blanched the veggies, then added a leafy rose-like centerpiece. To finish, a drizzle of TUK Olive Oil, fresh squeezed lemon juice, & very finely minced fresh garlic.

Fresh cauliflower on a bright white oval platter. So simple yet so elegant & appetizing. Steam cauliflower while sauteing fresh garlic in olive oil. Plate your cauliflower and drizzle the garlic & olive oil on top. This one is for my friend, Nancy.

The next time your bell peppers start to wilt, roast them! Remove all the seeds, slice, & make some delicious roasted peppers, either on the stove or your grill.

Coat in TUK Olive Oil or TUK Dressing.

I also love to pickle my own veggies with white vinegar. Boil 2 cups red or white vinegar with 1 cup of water. Let cool completely, wash your jars, add your veggies, then pour your cooled vinegar & water all the way to the top of each jar. Add TUK Dried Spices or fresh garlic, fennel seeds, or rosemary. Seal & refrigerate for 1-2 weeks. Then, I take out all the liquid but leave the veggies in their same containers & enjoy them for up to 2-3 months!

Homemade pickled bell peppers finished with TUK Dried Spices & TUK Dressing! Amazing!

ROASTED VEGGIES

When I roast veggies, I roast everything I have.
I use everything this earth gives us.

INGREDIENTS

Asparagus
Red onion
Carrot
Zucchini
Yellow squash
Plum tomato
White onion
Red onion
Eggplant

Pink salt & black pepper
TUK Dressing
TUK Olive Oil
TUK Dried Spices
Fresh herbs:
Mint

DIRECTIONS

Prepare a hot grill, griddle, or large stovetop pan. Wash & dry veggies completely with paper towel. Slice the way you like, any shape, just make sure all of them are about the same size. Chop fresh mint. Place all sliced veggies on a baking sheet lined with parchment paper. Brush all veggies in olive oil & use your hands to toss in order to completely coat in olive oil. Then, season well with dried spices.

At your grilling surface, grill each kind of veggie at one time. Grill your asparagus, set aside, grill your eggplant, set aside, and so on. Once off the grill, you are ready to assemble on your large, beautiful plate. Once you've assembled, drizzle olive oil & about 2-3 tbsp of dressing all over. Finish with your chopped fresh mint & a final dash of pink salt & black pepper.

Notes
I've also prepared this dish using celery, green onion, fennel, & brussels sprouts. I have even pre-steamed cauliflower, broccoli, & cabbage, sliced them all, & then grilled them. Pumpkin squash, too! Use any veggie you like. Open your imagination & what a beautiful plate you'll make!

STUFFED BABY PEPPERS

INGREDIENTS

4 mild Italian sausage
15-20 baby peppers, different colors!
1 shallot
2 whole eggs
2 baby peppers
1 cup green peas

1 cup parmigiano reggiano
1 cup breadcrumbs
Marinara Sauce
Pesto
Fresh Herbs:
Basil
Italian parsley

DIRECTIONS

Remove all seeds, stems, & pitting from all of your peppers. Finely chop two of the baby peppers and set aside. Finely chop your shallot & set aside. Finely chop your fresh parsley & set aside. Brown the sausage in a pan, place in a mixing bowl, & set aside.

Into the bowl of browned sausage, add your shallot, parsley, & small, diced peppers. In a separate small bowl, crack your two eggs, whisk, & add a pinch of pink salt, & then add to your sausage mixture. Add breadcrumbs & parmigiano reggiano. Add 1 teaspoon of pesto to the mixture.

Mix everything together now. Add more breadcrumbs if mixture is still too moist. Go ahead & prepare a large pan over medium heat. While that heats up, it's time to stuff your baby peppers! Take your mixture & stuff the peppers through their tops. Pack tightly. When your pan is hot & ready, add a nice layer of marinara to the pan. Once simmering, gently lay all of your peppers, stuffing side facing outward. Once simmering for a few minutes, add green peas and let cook for a few minutes.

Then, garnish with large leaves of fresh basil on top of your peppers for the final simmer.

Serve & enjoy!

STUFFED ZUCCHINI & EGGPLANT

INGREDIENTS

6 large zucchini or 3 eggplant
1 white onion
1-2 cups small mushrooms
2 whole eggs
3 cloves fresh garlic
½ lb ground pork
½ lb ground beef
1 cup pecorino romano
2 cups breadcrumbs
Pink salt & black pepper
Fresh herbs:
Italian parsley

DIRECTIONS

Preheat your oven to 350F.

Cut zucchini in half, long ways, & then cut again in half, short ways. Scoop out all seeds & membranes & place in a mixing bowl. Chop white onion & mushroom & combine. Mince parsley. Mince garlic. Prepare a pan over medium heat.

To your hot pan, add a few tbsp of olive oil. When ready, add your onion, mushroom, & the insides from the zucchini. Once fully sauted, remove from heat & set aside. Brown your beef & pork for about five minutes & drain all fat.

Once the meat & veggie mixtures have both cooled, combine & add pecorino romano, pink salt & black pepper, garlic, ½ cup minced parsley, & breadcrumbs. Mix again. Last, mix in the two eggs. This is now your stuffing! Use a spoon to fill your zucchini boats.

Bake at 350F for at least 30 minutes or until zucchini stuffing browns nicely on top.

Notes
This same recipe can be followed for stuffed eggplant.
However, be sure to roast your eggplant prior to adding stuffing.

PANE

OVERNIGHT DOUGH

Here it is! An easy, multi-purpose dough that you can use for all things 'bread,' pizza, & more. This dough requires 12-24 hours.

INGREDIENTS

3 cups all-purpose, strong white bread flour, sifted
2 ¼ tsp active dry yeast
1 tbsp raw cane sugar

1 cup warm water @ 110F
3 tbsp TUK Olive Oil
1 tsp pink salt

DIRECTIONS

First, in a measuring cup, combine yeast, sugar, & warm water. Mix thoroughly.

Sift your flour to yield at least 3 cups of flour. You may not use all of it but at least you'll have it available. Add flour to a mixing bowl. Add your salt.

Begin to form your dough. Use your hands to combine, stretch, & knead. When your dough is almost formed, add your olive oil. Then, finish up kneading your dough.

As needed, you can use more water but it must also be 110F. You can also use more flour if needed. You should need to work your dough for at least 10 minutes in order to yield a nice, soft dough. Dough should not stick to your hands.

When dough is done, brush a large bowl with olive oil and add your dough. Wrap in plastic wrap, add to a large plastic bag, & place in the refrigerator for 24 hours.

After 24 hours, remove dough from the refrigerator. Cover in kitchen towels for 2-3 hours before using your dough. Your overnight dough needs to rise & reach room temperature before you can use your dough.

30-MINUTE DOUGH

Okay, here's the quick dough.
If you want to make a focaccia today, this is the recipe you want!

INGREDIENTS

3 cups all-purpose, strong white bread flour, sifted
2 ¼ tsp fast rise yeast
1 ½ tsp raw cane sugar

1 cup warm water @ 110F
3 tbsp TUK Olive Oil
Pink salt

DIRECTIONS

First, in a measuring cup, combine yeast, sugar, & warm water. Mix thoroughly.

Sift your flour to yield at least 3 cups of flour. You may not use all of it but at least you'll have it available. Add flour to a mixing bowl. Add a little less than 1 tbsp of pink salt.

Begin to form your dough. Use your hands to combine, stretch, & knead. When your dough is almost formed, add your olive oil. Then, finish up kneading your dough.

As needed, you can use more water but it must also be 110F. You can also use more flour if needed. You should need to work your dough for at least 10 minutes in order to yield a nice, soft dough. Dough should not stick to your hands.

When dough is done, brush a large bowl with olive oil and add your dough. Wrap in plastic wrap, secure with a plastic bag, and cover with a few kitchen towels. The warmer the dough can get, the better.

Let rest for 30 minutes. Now, you can make some delicious focaccia, pizza, zeppole, anything!

Another great activity to do with your family...make homemade focaccia!

As my grandson has grown up, I am amazed. Every time he walks into my kitchen, he takes over! I love it.

THE FOCACCIA

with kalamata olives, tomatoes, & fresh rosemary.

INGREDIENTS

1 dough
½ cup all-purpose flour
1 cup kalamata olives
1 cup tomato of your choice
3 cloves fresh garlic

TUK Olive Oil
½ cup parmigiano reggiano
Pink salt & black pepper
Fresh herbs:
Rosemary

DIRECTIONS

First, allow your dough to rise & reach room temperature. So, take your dough, place in a lightly oiled bowl and cover with a few kitchen towels. Let rest until it has reached room temperature.

Meanwhile, preheat oven to 475F.

Remove all seeds & juice from tomatoes & dice. (Remember, if using cherry tomatoes, you don't need to do this step.) Then, chop olives, rosemary, & garlic.

When dough is ready, lightly flour your work surface & begin to stretch & flatten your dough. Lightly oil a baking sheet & place your dough on top. Stretch to fill the baking sheet. Then, wet your fingers a little & press indentations into the dough. These make great places for the olive oil & toppings to nestle into.

Drizzle olive oil all over! Then, move the pan around to let the olive oil spread. Add kalamata olives, tomatoes, parmigiano reggiano, & rosemary. Finish with pink salt & black pepper.

Bake at 475F for 10-15 minutes on the top rack. Watch closely as the top of the focaccia bakes quickly.

'Pizzettes with Melina'

Here, I am making pizzettes with Melina, my granddaughter! Here, she's using a miniature cast iron skillet for her pizzette. Have fun, use your imagination, & top your pizzettes with any toppings you like! Also, to parents, grandparents, aunts, & uncles, what a fun activity to do with the children in your lives!

PIZZETTE

INGREDIENTS

1 dough
Fresh mozzarella
TUK Olive Oil

Sauce, toppings, & fresh herbs of your choice!

DIRECTIONS

Prepare a small frying pan over medium-high heat. Break up your dough into about 4 quarters to make 4 pizzettes.

To your really hot pan, brush a little olive oil, & place your raw dough. Fry until crispy. Then, pick up, brush more olive oil on the pan, & cook the other side. Brush some more oil on the top of your pizzette, add sauce, mozzarella, & toppings of your choice.

Cover your pizzette until the top is warm and melted & enjoy!

STUFFED BREAD

INGREDIENTS

1 dough
1 bundle of rapini
3 cloves fresh garlic
TUK Olive Oil

½ cup parmigiano reggiano
½ cup provolone
Pink salt & black pepper

DIRECTIONS

Preheat your oven to 425F & allow your dough to rise & reach room temperature.

Bring a pot of salted water to a boil & cook your rapini. Brush a large baking sheet with olive oil. Stretch your dough & lay on baking sheet. Rough chop your garlic & cut some slices of provolone.

Once softened, remove rapini & squeeze out all water. Lay rapini beautifully across your pizza dough. Add parmigiano reggiano, provolone, garlic, pink salt, black pepper, & a drizzle of deliciousness...olive oil!

Now, begin to roll your dough from the long edge. Pat down & secure tightly as you are rolling. Once rolled, make sure your bread is completely sealed. Flatten the bread just a little & brush with olive oil. Make 1 inch slits about 2 inches apart from each other, end to end.

Bake at 425F for at least 30 minutes or until golden with a slightly crispy top. Let rest before cutting into your stuffed bread.

for Franca

INSALATA

for Dan

BEET SALAD

INGREDIENTS

3 raw beets
1 red onion
2 cups arugula

TUK Dressing
TUK Dried Spices
Pink salt & black pepper
Fresh herbs:
Italian parsley

DIRECTIONS

Bring a pot of water to a boil. Meanwhile, wash & peel your beets and then cut in half. Chop red onion & parsley to your size preference, combine in a bowl, & set aside.

Once water is boiling, add your halved beets to the water. Cook thoroughly until tender. If making the salad now, you can add your cooked beets to a bowl of ice water to cool. If making the salad later, let beets cool & refrigerate until you're ready to use.

Jar beets & onion in white vinegar for 30 minutes to an hour before assembling. Drain before using. Slice beets into size of your preference. Then, mix in to your red onion & parsley. Add about ¼ cup of dressing, pink salt, black pepper, & a dash of dried spices.

Once your beet mixture is complete, add on top of a bed of rich arugula.

CHOPPED SALAD

INGREDIENTS

Hearts of romaine
Hearts of celery
Head of fennel

1 carrot, pickled
1 red onion, pickled
TUK Dressing

DIRECTIONS

Chop red onion into long curled slices. Prepare a pickling jar with white vinegar & a little bit of pink salt, just like a marinade. Add your onions & seal tightly.

Chop carrots into small circles or sticks. Prepare another pickling jar with white vinegar & pink salt and do the same thing for the carrots. Add your carrots & seal tightly.

For a quicker salad, let the onion & carrot pickle for 1-2 hours. You can let them pickle longer or even overnight for a salad preparation in advance.

When ready to assemble your salad, chop hearts of romaine, celery, & fennel. Add your pickled red onions & carrots. Finish with TUK Dressing. So refreshing!

A bed of romaine, spinach, & arugula topped with fresh fruits & veggies. Peeled apple slices, crisp radish, ripe blueberries & bright red cherry tomatoes, shaved carrot, & kalamata olives. In the center, we decorate with strawberries just because! Why not? You can top with gorgonzola, bleu cheese, or whatever is your favorite.

A scalloped platter with romaine, spinach, & mixed greens. White onion with circles of cucumber & carrot. Diced tangerine & cherry tomato, with a centerpiece of green & orange.

MANGO & BLUEBERRY SALAD

INGREDIENTS

Mixed greens
2 mangoes, ripe but firm
1 cup blueberries
Juice of ½ lemon

1 tsp dijon mustard
3 tbsp of your local honey
¼ cup TUK Olive Oil
Pink salt & black pepper

DIRECTIONS

Prepare a large platter with a bed of your mixed greens. For this recipe, I like to use arugula, baby spinach, & of course, dandelion!

Long slice your mangoes.

And now, let's make a salad dressing. Start with the dijon mustard and a fork. Just whisk it by itself first. Then, add your oil & lemon juice while still whisking with your fork. Still whisking, add pink salt & black pepper. Whisk more and then add your honey. Whisk thoroughly & then taste! If too dense, add a teaspoon of water. The consistency should drizzle straight through a fork & should not stick. Add a teaspoon of water at a time until you reach the right consistency. Finish the dressing with pink salt & black pepper to taste.

Plate mangoes generously on the bed of mixed greens. Drizzle your homemade salad dressing & decorate your plate with fresh blueberries.

Before you throw away those bell peppers, let's make a salad! Roast or pickle your yellow & orange bell peppers. Prepare a bed of mixed greens. Add slices of peppers, red cherry tomatoes, & place a large pearl of bufala mozzarella in the middle. So good! Then, drizzle with TUK Dressing & a dash of TUK Dried Spices.

A large white platter, of course, to serve all my family & friends! Start with a bed of fresh greens, using romaine hearts, rich arugula, & dandelion. Then, add ripe d'anjou pear, crisp radish, & pomegranate seeds. Build your centerpiece & finish with your favorite dressing. Another one of Sara's spontaneous kitchen creations. How will you make yours?

RADICCHIO

This recipe is great for a large group of people where you want to serve each of your guests with their own elegant & unique salad.

INGREDIENTS

1 head of radicchio
2 cups dandelion
2 cups baby spinach
5 hearts of celery
A few baby cucumbers

Carrot & apple
Orange or tangerine
Lemon
TUK Olive Oil
Pink salt & black pepper
Fresh herbs:
Fennel

DIRECTIONS

Set aside your radicchio. Set aside a few baby spinach & dandelion. Into a very small dice, chop celery, cucumbers, some dandelion and spinach, & mix all together. Chop fennel into very fine pieces. Prepare a few slices of apple, orange, and/or tangerine.

Take leaves of radicchio & make into a flower shape for each individual salad. Then, make a bed of dandelion & baby spinach on the bottom of each radicchio. Then, fill with your mixed veggies.

Garnish on top with larger slices of your fruit & any remaining veggie to decorate. Top it off with a squeeze of fresh lemon juice, a drizzle of olive oil, sprinkle your thin, green fennel pieces, & finish with pink salt, black pepper, & a squeeze of lemon juice.

BISCOTTI AL LIMONE
lemon cookies

INGREDIENTS

4 whole eggs
400g sifted all-purpose flour
100g raw cane sugar
¼ cup powdered sugar

1 tbsp vanilla extract
1 tbsp lemon zest
Juice of ½ large lemon
½ cup TUK Olive Oil

DIRECTIONS

Preheat oven to 350F. Sift flour to create 400g of sifted flour. Zest & juice lemon. Keep separate & set aside.

First, mix eggs, sugar, & vanilla together. Then, add lemon juice, lemon zest, & ¼ cup olive oil. Mix. Next, slowly add in your flour while mixing simultaneously. Now, you have your cookie dough!

Next, coat your hands in powdered sugar. By the spoonful, add cookie dough to your hands to make a cookie shape. Form all cookies.

To a cookie sheet, brush olive oil where you are going to place each of your cookies. Then, top each oiled spot with powdered sugar. Place all cookies directly on those spots. Then, sprinkle powdered sugar on top of your cookies.

Bake at 350F for 8-10 minutes or until lightly golden. They should still be soft when you remove them from the oven.

Notes
Make a little crispier if you want to dip in coffee!
Sometimes that's what I like to do.

BISCOTTI DI MANDORLA
almond biscotti

INGREDIENTS

4 whole eggs
600g sifted all-purpose flour
430g raw cane sugar
12g salted, softened butter

250g ground almonds
12g leavening agent for baking
Pink salt

DIRECTIONS

Preheat oven to 350F. Prepare a baking sheet with parchment paper.

With just a pinch of pink salt, mix all ingredients together to form a ball of dough.

Flour your work surface & shape your dough into a loaf. Cut loaf into 4 pieces. Then, shape them into loaves, too.

Add biscotti loaves to baking sheet and bake at 350F for 30 minutes.

Your loaves should still be soft after 30 minutes.
Turn oven OFF.
Remove loaves from oven & let cool.

Once cool, slice into individual biscotti, lay flat, & put back into 'OFF' oven. Let crisp for about 5 minutes. Watch them to make sure they do not get too dark.

Enjoy with your morning coffee...or dip!

BOM BOMS

One of Sara's Unexpected Creations!

INGREDIENTS

½ cup water
1 cup heavy whipping cream
½ cup powdered sugar

2 cups cocoa powder
1 cup semi-sweet chocolate chips
1 cup shaved coconut
1 cup sliced almonds

DIRECTIONS

Prepare a pan over low-medium heat. Prepare a cookie sheet with optional parchment paper. Coat cookie sheet or paper with a layer of powdered sugar.

With the exception of powdered sugar, melt all ingredients together in hot pan & mix slowly.

Coat your hands with powdered sugar. By the spoonful, add to your hands & roll into a ball. Then, roll each ball into powdered sugar & place onto your cookie sheet.

Let your 'bom boms' rest & then enjoy!

PAN DI SPAGNA

sponge cake

INGREDIENTS

2 whole eggs
4 egg whites
¼ cup all-purpose flour
½ tsp baking powder
1 cup raw cane sugar
¼ cup powdered sugar

Pink salt
Optional:
Homemade whipped cream
Fresh strawberries

DIRECTIONS

Preheat your oven to 350F. Prepare a cake tin with parchment paper, leaving no tin edges exposed. Sift your flour. Whisk all eggs in a mixing bowl. Then, add sugar. Beat mixture for 15 minutes continuously, do not stop.

Add a pinch of pink salt & keep mixing. Add baking powder & keep mixing. Once you reach the color & consistency of pancake batter, add sifted flour slowly while gently folding into your batter.

Once batter runs smooth, add to your cake tin.

Bake at 350F for 35 minutes.

Add powdered sugar or whipping cream with fresh strawberries. Enjoy in the morning with your coffee. So delicious!

ELEGANT CREPES

INGREDIENTS

4 whole eggs
1 cup all-purpose flour
1 cup milk
½ cup raw sugar
¼ tsp pure vanilla
OR ¼ tsp lemon extract

Zest of ¼ lemon
1 tsp squeezed lemon juice
1 tsp TUK Olive Oil
3 tsp salted butter

Yield: 10 crepes

DIRECTIONS

Prepare a 9-inch pan over low-medium heat. With an electric mixer, beat eggs, flour, milk, pure vanilla/lemon extract, lemon zest, & sugar in a bowl. This mixture is now your crepe batter!

Mix olive oil with butter in a small dish. Brush your hot pan with olive oil & butter mixture. Make sure you get the sides, too.

Using a ⅓ measuring cup, pour batter into pan. Tilt the pan & go around in a circle to make sure the crepe mixture fills the whole pan in a nice, thin layer. The bottom of the crepe will have light brown spots when it's ready to be turned over. It should be about a minute to cook each side. Turn over with a fork.

As needed, move the pan on & off of heat to keep from sticking. Heat must stay at the same temperature for all crepes. Re-oil your pan, edges included, after every third crepe. Stack your crepes & prepare to fill.

Notes
Your first crepe will always be the worst.
Also, if you have extra crepes than needed, freeze them!
Secure them & lay flat in the freezer for later.

APPLE CREPE FILLING

*You can use these crepe filling recipes as templates
for other crepe fillings using other fruits that you enjoy.*

INGREDIENTS

5 sweet apples
Juice of ½ lemon

2 tsp raw cane sugar
2 tsp salted butter

DIRECTIONS

Peel apples & cut into slices. Prepare a pan over medium heat.

Place butter in hot pan & add apples. Add sugar & lemon juice. Pan should begin to sizzle.

Cook until apple filling thickens to a consistency of your liking.

Fill your crepes with your apple filling & drizzle any excess apple over the top.

STRAWBERRY CREPE FILLING

INGREDIENTS

1 pint strawberries

1 tsp fresh lemon juice

2-3 tbsp raw cane sugar

2 tbsp salted butter

DIRECTIONS

Discard stems from strawberries, then slice. Prepare a pan over medium heat.

To your hot pan, add butter. Then, add all ingredients to thicken.

Once thickened to your liking, fill your crepes with this delicious strawberry filling!

MANGO CREPE DRIZZLE

Here is an idea for a finishing touch on your elegant homemade crepes.

INGREDIENTS

2 ripe mangoes
1 tsp fresh lemon juice

3 tbsp raw sugar
2 tbsp salted butter

DIRECTIONS

Prepare a pan over medium heat. Peel & slice mangoes.

Place butter onto hot pan. Add sugar, mango, & lemon juice. Cook to thicken.

Once thickened to a desirable consistency, place in a blender with just a splash of rum for added flavor. A little goes a long way though, so don't add too much.

Now, you have a delicious mango sauce to drizzle on top of your crepes.

TIRAMISU

INGREDIENTS

1 cup soft mascarpone
½ cup heavy whipping cream
1 pack of ladyfinger cookies

2-3 cups brewed espresso
OR ½ cup spiced rum
1 tsp vanilla extract
1 tsp brandy or amaretto

DIRECTIONS

First, if using espresso, brew your espresso to yield about 2-3 cups, just to make sure you have enough. Next, whip your heavy whipping cream about halfway to whipped cream. Add mascarpone to your whipped cream & continue to whip. Now, add sugar, vanilla, & brandy or amaretto.

Soak ladyfingers directly in your brewed espresso OR 1/2 cup spiced rum, only for a few moments.

Layer a 9x13 dish with soaked ladyfingers followed by a layer of cream. Repeat for two total layers.

And there you have your very own homemade tiramisu!

MACEDONIA DI FRUTTA

Italians? We are very slow to get to dessert after having such big meals. So, having fruit is very refreshing. There is no correct recipe for this. First, use your imagination. Picture what's in your Macedonia di Frutta. Picture your favorite fruits. Then, go do it! For me, I picture this beautiful glass on a stand. And then I use all the fruits that I love or even just what I have that day.
Use what you love when you make Macedonia di Frutta your way.

INGREDIENTS

2-3 firm lemons, thick rind
Zest from all lemons
Juice from all lemons
Homemade whipped cream
Champagne or liqueur, like sweet vermouth, cognac, or rum, but **never** coffee liqueur
Raw cane sugar

All the fruit you want! Like, berries, grapes, bananas, cherries, apples, peaches, kiwi, anything **except** watermelon!
Fresh herbs:
Mint

DIRECTIONS

Chop all of your fruit into any shape & size you like. However, keep all the same size, relatively. Add to a large bowl. Chop *a lot* of fresh mint. Then, depending on how much fruit you are using, add 1-2 tbsp of raw cane sugar, lemon juice, lemon zest, & chopped mint.

Next, give your macedonia di frutta a little swing. I like to use cognac or rum. Sara goes crazy mixing things up, you know that. So go ahead & add the refreshing swing of your choice. Mix all together but very gently. Keep all fruit intact.

Refrigerate for at least two hours...let it get drunker! Overnight is best.

When you're ready to enjoy, display in a large glass bowl so you can see all of your beautiful, colorful fruits. Add more mint all over. Serve in small glass dessert dishes or even stemware. Whip up some fresh whipped cream & add a spoonful on top. Serve with biscotti & lastly, a sprig of fresh mint. *Amazing!*

THREE CHOCOLATE CAKE
"It's like going to heaven and coming back." - Kathy

INGREDIENTS

2 whole eggs
150g white granulated sugar
125g sweet cream butter
220g all-purpose flour
2 ¼ tsp leavening agent for baking
1 tsp vanilla extract

250ml whole milk
20g cocoa powder
20g powdered sugar
200g dark baking chocolate bar
1 bag semi-sweet chocolate chips

DIRECTIONS

Preheat your oven to 350F. For this recipe, you will need a springform cake pan.

With an electric mixer, mix sugar & eggs. Keep mixing while slowly adding milk. Keep mixing while adding a spoonful at a time of flour, very slowly, or as we say, "poco poco." Next, add powdered sugar.

In a separate small bowl, add cocoa powder & leavening agent together. Then, add this mixture to the big bowl. This is now your three chocolate cake mixture!

Cut out a piece of parchment paper to cover the bottom of your cake pan. Wet the parchment paper & place on the bottom so it sticks to the pan. Butter the circular edge of the cake pan & then flour it. Pour your cake mixture into the pan.

Chop ½ of your dark chocolate bar into pieces & pour on top. Then, add the whole bag of chocolate chips.

Bake at 350F on the center rack for at least 20 minutes. Test with a toothpick until it runs clean. Once your cake is out of the oven, unlock & plate your cake. It's now time for the final step.

With the other half of your dark chocolate bar, create or use a double boiler at your stove to melt the chocolate. Then, pour this melted chocolate all over your cake. Assemble with fresh strawberries, powdered sugar, or whichever toppings you like.

ZEPPOLE

INGREDIENTS

1 dough
¼ cup all-purpose flour
1 cup warm water
½ cup canola oil
½ cup TUK Olive Oil

2 cups powdered sugar
Cocoa powder
Raw local honey

DIRECTIONS

First, allow your dough to rise & reach room temperature before using.

Prepare a frying pan over medium heat.

Put powdered sugar in a mixing bowl. Make some chocolate sauce using your cocoa powder, just follow the instructions on the container. Last, pour a little flour on your work surface.

To your hot frying pan, add your olive & canola oils. Lightly wet your hands. Pull your dough into pieces, each piece just long enough to make a donut shape...or any shape you like! Roll each piece, one at a time, into the flour to fully coat. Then, pick up each piece of dough with tongs & place gently into your frying pan. Make sure each piece is completely covered in oil. Add as many zeppole to your pan as can fit without touching. Fry until golden on each side, about 3 minutes per side. When ready, remove from the oil onto a bed of paper towels to drain the excess oil and cool. Once you have all your zeppole, time to flavor!

Options: Drizzle raw honey & cinnamon on top. Or, coat with powdered sugar. Or even better, coat with chocolate & then powdered sugar!

Sara Ciliberto is the owner of *The Unexpected Kitchen, LLC.* This is her debut cookbook! You can purchase her dried spices, olive oils & more at her website. Join her cooking show on Facebook Live with viewers from all around the world. Follow for show updates, mouth-watering photos, and Sara's daily creativity! Look out for Sara's short-form videos, where she walks you through an entire recipe from start to finish so you can follow along in your own kitchen!

For media & professional inquiries ::
theunexpectedkitchen@gmail.com
Website :: www.theunexpectedkitchen.com
Facebook :: The Unexpected Kitchen
YouTube :: The Unexpected Kitchen
Instagram :: the_unexpected_kitchen
TikTok :: the_unexpected_kitchen

Thank you for supporting my debut cookbook,
& to each and every one of you who got me here.

Cin cin!
-Sara Ciliberto

www.ingramcontent.com/pod-product-compliance
Lightning Source LLC
Chambersburg PA
CBHW060812010526
44117CB00002B/13